THE BIGGEST BOOK OF JOKES

OVER 2000 JOKES

Illustrated By
Glen Singleton

hinkler

Published by Hinkler Books Pty Ltd
45–55 Fairchild Street
Heatherton Victoria 3202 Australia
www.hinkler.com.au

hinkler

© Hinkler Books Pty Ltd 2011

Cover and text design: Pandemonium Creative
Typesetting: MPS Limited
Prepress: Splitting Image

ISBN: 978 1 7418 4768 0

Printed and bound in China

Contents

WHAT DO YOU GET . . . ?

What do you get when you cross a doctor with a comedian?
A surgeon who has their patients in stitches.

What do you get when you cross a baby rabbit with a vegetable?
A bunion.

What do you get when you cross an elephant with a rhino?
Elifino.

What do you get when you cross a bridge with a car?
To the other side of the river.

What do you get when you cross a criminal with a rubbish collector?
Organised grime.

What do you get when you cross a skunk with a table tennis ball?
Ping-pong.

What do you get when you cross a snake with a builder?
A boa constructor.

What do you get when you cross a book with some perfume?
A best smeller.

What do you get when you cross a vampire with a dwarf?
A monster that sucks blood out of people's kneecaps.

What do you get when you cross a flower with a fool?
A blooming idiot.

What do you get when you cross a bear with a cow?
Winnie the Moo.

What do you get when you cross a hairdresser with a surfer?
Permanent waves.

What do you get when you cross a nun with a chicken?
A pecking order.

What do you get when you cross a seagull with a pair of wheels?
A bi-seagull.

What do you get when you cross a hippopotamus with someone who is always sick?
A hippochondriac.

What do you get when you cross a plumber with a ballerina?
A tap dancer.

What do you get when you cross a flower with a big cat who wears a cravat?
A dandelion.

What do you get when you cross a dinosaur with a computer?
A mega-bite.

What do you get when you cross a kookaburra with a jug of gravy?
A laughing stock.

What do you get when you cross an English king with a fireplace?
Alfred the Grate.

What do you get when you cross a black bird with a madman?
A raven lunatic.

What do you get when you cross a cow with a clairvoyant?
A message from the udder side.

What do you get when you cross an Apple computer with fast food?
A Big Mac.

What do you get when you cross an overheating Apple computer with fast food?
A Big Mac and fries.

What do you get when you cross a bushranger with a dessert?
Ned Jelly.

What do you get when you cross a shark with a crocodile with a Tyrannosaurus Rex?
I don't know, but don't take it swimming.

What do you get when you cross a mouse with an orange?
A pipsqueak.

What do you get when you cross a mouse and a deer?
Mickey Moose.

What do you get when you cross a sheep with a radiator?
Central bleating.

What do you get when you cross a skunk with an owl?
A bird who stinks but doesn't give a hoot.

What do you get when you cross a plane with some pastry?
Pie in the sky.

Someone suggested a game of 'HERE COMES THE LION' at Jumbo's 3rd Birthday party startling his 2 ton friends into a stampede.

What do you get when you cross an elephant with a cake?
Crumbs.

What do you get when you cross a cow with a whale?
Mooby dick.

What do you get when you cross a cow with a duck?
Cream quackers.

What do you get when you cross a painter with a police officer?
A brush with the law.

What do you get when you cross an elephant with a bottle of rum?
Trunk and disorderly.

What do you get when you cross a hare with a walking stick?
A hurry-cane (hurricane).

What do you get when you cross a frog with a Native American?
A toadempole.

What do you get when you cross a flea with a comedian?
A nitwit.

What do you get when you cross a police officer with a ghost?
An inspectre.

What do you get when you cross a kangaroo with a skyscraper?
A high jumper.

I think I could see the Police Station ceiling in a nice cool lime green with pink trim...

What do you get when you cross a witch and a skunk?
An ugly smell.

What do you get when you cross a snowman with a Cuban?
An ice cube.

What do you get when you cross a master criminal with a fish?
The Codfather.

What do you get when you cross a watch with a parrot?
Politicks.

What do you get when you cross a chicken with a cement mixer?
A bricklayer.

What do you get when you cross a jungle animal with an accountant?
A wild bore.

What do you get when you cross a parrot with a soldier?
A parrot trooper.

What do you get when you cross a heater with a witch?
A hot spell.

What do you get when you cross a wedding with a cliff?
A marriage that is on the rocks.

DUMB & DUMBER

A fool went to the train station.
Fool: *'I'd like a return ticket please.'*
Ticket seller: *'Certainly sir, where to?'*
Fool: *'Back here of course.'*

Did you hear about the crazy hitchhiker?
He got up early so there wouldn't be much traffic around.

You're so dumb, when you eat M&Ms, you throw out the Ws.

My girlfriend talks so much that when she goes on holidays, she has to spread suntan lotion on her tongue!

Did you hear about the fool who hijacked a submarine?
He demanded $2 million dollars and a parachute.

How many toes does a fool have?
Take off your socks and count them.

Did you hear about the crazy cyclist who won the Tour de France?
He did a lap of honour.

Did you hear about the farmer's boy who hated the country?
He went to the big city and got a job as a shoeshine boy, and so the farmer made hay while the son shone.

George knocked on the door of his friend's house.
When his friend's mother answered he asked, *'Can Albert come out to play?'*
'No,' said Albert's mother. *'It's too cold.'*
'Well then,' said George, *'can his football come out to play?'*

Robert was a fool – he saw a sign outside a police station that read: 'Man Wanted For Robbery,' so he went in and applied for the job!

What do you call a fool with half a brain?
A genius.

Stop! This is a one-way street.
Well, I'm only going one way!

'*So you took your medicine right after your bath?*' the doctor asked his crazy patient.
'*No, doctor,*' replied the fool. '*By the time I'd drunk the bath, I had no room left for the medicine!*'

The teacher told the crazy fool she knew he'd skipped school last Friday, and heard he'd been playing games at the arcade.
The fool told her it wasn't true – and he had the baseball game tickets to prove it!

Did you hear about the fool who spent two hours in a department store?
He was looking for a cap with a peak at the back.

Did you hear about the fool who went waterskiing?
He spent his whole holiday looking for a sloping lake.

Did you hear about the crazy sailor who was discharged from his submarine duties?
He was found sleeping with the window open.

How do you milk a mouse?
You can't. The bucket won't fit under it.

Did you hear about the silly glass blower?
He inhaled and got a pane in the tummy.

Why did the crazy sailor grab some soap when his ship sank?
Because he thought he would wash ashore.

Did you hear about the crazy photographer?
He saved used light bulbs for his dark room.

Did you hear about the fool who wanted value for money?
He sat at the back of the bus to get a longer ride.

Why did the fool get 17 of his friends to accompany him to the movies?
Because he'd heard it was not for under-18s.

Did you hear about the fool who stole a calendar?
He got 12 months.

How did the fool burn his ear?
He was ironing when the phone rang.

What about the fool who burnt both his ears?
The caller rang back.

Why did the fool put on a red coat and top hat and carry a telephone line under his arm?
He thought he had been invited to go fax hunting.

The gangland boss was surprised to find one of his gang sawing the legs off his bed.
'Why are you doing that?' he asked.
'Well, you did ask me to lie low for a bit,' the fool replied.

Have you heard about the fool who went into a 24-hour store and asked what time they closed?

Did you hear about the fool who locked his keys in the car?
He called a mechanic to get his family out.

'*Your finger is in my soup bowl!*' said the man.
'*Don't worry,*' said the foolish waiter. '*The soup isn't hot.*'

What did the foolish window cleaner have on the top of his ladder?
A stop sign.

Did you hear about the foolish glazier who tried to fit a new window?
He broke it with a hammer.

Why did the fool walk into the electricity company with a $20 note in each ear?
Because he'd received a bill saying he was $40 in arrears.

Susie asked the fool if his tent leaked when he was camping.
'*Only when it rained,*' he said.

'*Are you lost?*' the policeman asked the silly schoolgirl.
'*Of course not,*' she replied. '*I'm here, it's my school that's lost.*'

Have you heard about the fool who thinks a fjord is a Scandinavian car?

Why did the fool take a gun with him on his white-water rafting holiday?
So he could shoot the rapids.

Did you hear about the fool who went on a package tour near where the brain-eating headhunters live?
He was the only survivor.

A crazy bank robber rushes into a bank, points two fingers at the teller and says, '*This is a muck-up.*'
'*Don't you mean a stick-up?*' said the teller.
'*No. It's a muck-up,*' replied the robber. '*I've forgotten my gun!*'

When the fool's co-worker asked why he had a sausage stuck behind his ear, he replied, '*Oh… I must have eaten my pencil for lunch!*'

A perfect landing

WALLY-AIR

Why did the foolish pilot land his plane on a house?
Because they'd left the landing lights on.

Did you hear about the bungee jumper who shot up and down for 3 hours before they could bring him under control?
He had a yo-yo in his pocket.

A fool was just about to dive into a pool when a lifesaver came rushing up.
Lifesaver: *'Don't jump. There's no water in the pool.'*
Fool: *'It's okay. I can't swim.'*

How do you get a one-armed fool out of a tree?
Wave to him.

Did you hear about the fool who went skiing?
He skied up the slope and caught the chair lift down.

How many fools does it take to change a light bulb?
Five, one to climb the ladder, the others to turn the ladder around and around.

Did you hear about the foolish water polo player?
His horse drowned.

Why do foolish workers only get a half-hour lunch break?
Because if they took any longer, they would have to be re-trained.

How do you compliment a fool?
Tell him he has an open mind.

Did you hear about the foolish firing squad?
They stood in a circle.

Did you hear about the foolish karate champion who joined the army?
The first time he saluted, he nearly killed himself.

ATTENN-SHUNNN!
WAK:

Why did the team of fools always lose the tug-of-war?
They pushed.

Why did the fool leap out the window?
To try his new jump suit.

Wally, what's the weather like?
I don't know. It's too foggy to tell.

Did you hear about the foolish burglar?
He robbed a music store and stole the lute.

What do foolish kids do at Halloween?
They carve a face on an apple and go bobbing for pumpkins.

Why did the fool quit his job as a telephonist?
Because he kept hearing voices.

Did you hear about the foolish helicopter pilot?
He switched off the propeller because he couldn't stand the draft.

Did you hear about the foolish terrorist who was told to blow up a car?
He burnt his mouth on the exhaust pipe.

Why did the fool drive into the river?
He was trying to dip his headlights.

Why do fools always have stupid grins on their faces?
Because they're stupid.

What do you do if a fool throws a hand grenade at you?
Pull the pin and throw it back.

How does a fool call his dog?
He puts two fingers in his mouth and shouts 'Rover!'

'Mum, can I please change my name right now?' asked Ben.

'Why would you want to do that, dear?' asked his mum.

'Because Dad says he's going to spank me, as sure as my name's Benjamin!'

Did you hear about the silly pirate?
He had a patch over both eyes.

You are so dumb you take your bicycle to bed because you don't want to walk in your sleep.

Why did the fool throw away his donut?
Because it had a hole in the middle.

Did you hear about the foolish shoplifter?
He hurt his back trying to lift the corner store.

Did you hear about the other foolish shoplifter?
He stole a free sample.

Did you hear about the silly school kid who was studying Greek Mythology?
When the teacher asked him to name something that was half-man and half-beast he replied, 'Buffalo Bill.'

Did you hear about the silly secretary?
She was so good she could type 60 mistakes a minute!

Did you hear about the foolish shoe repairman?
A customer gave him a pair of shoes to be soled, so he sold them.

Did you hear about the fool who had a brain transplant?
The brain rejected him.

How do you stop a dog doing his business in the hall?
Put him outside.

Do you turn on your computer with your left hand or your right hand?
My right hand.
Amazing! Most people have to use the on/off switch!

May I try on that dress in the window?
No. I'm afraid you'll have to use the dressing room like everyone else.

You're not as stupid as you look. That would be impossible.

Mum, I'm not going to school today.
Why not?
Because it's Sunday.

You're so dumb, you took your mobile phone back to the shop because it came without a cord.

Why was the Egyptian girl worried?
Because her Daddy was a Mummy!

Why did the dinosaur fall out of a palm tree?
Because a hippopotamus pushed him out.

Dad was taking Danny around the museum, when they came across a magnificent stuffed lion in a case.
'Dad,' asked a puzzled Danny. *'How did they shoot the lion without breaking the glass?'*

Mum, Mum, Dad's broken my computer!
How did he do that?
I dropped it in on his head!

Dad: *'Don't be selfish. Let your brother use the sled half the time.'*
Son: *'I do, Dad. I use it going down the hill and he gets to use it coming up the hill!'*

Emma: *'What a cool pair of odd socks you have on, Jill.'*

Jill: *'Yes, and I have another pair just like it at home.'*

Why did the foolish farmer pack up and move to the city?
Because he'd heard that the country was at war.

Three men were sentenced to death by firing squad. Just as they applied the blindfold to the first man, he yelled, *'CYCLONE.'* In the confusion, he escaped. Just as they applied the blindfold to the second man, he yelled, *'FLOOD.'* In the confusion, he escaped. The third man was a bit of a fool. Just as they applied the blindfold to him, he yelled out, *'FIRE.'*

Two fools were walking home one night.
Fool 1: *'Is that the sun or the moon?'*
Fool 2: *'I don't know, I don't live around here.'*

You're so dumb, it takes you an hour to cook one-minute noodles.

You are so dumb you can't pass a blood test.

Customer: *'I cleaned my computer and now it doesn't work.'*
Repairman: *'What did you clean it with?'*
Customer: *'Soap and water.'*
Repairman: *'Water's never meant to get near a computer!'*
Customer: *'Oh, I bet it wasn't the water that caused the problem . . . it was when I put it in the spin dryer!'*

You're so slow, you can't even catch your breath.

'Why are you crying, Ted?' asked his mum.
'Because my new sneakers hurt,' Ted replied.
'That's because you've put them on the wrong feet.'
'But they're the only feet I have!'

What do you call a top girl-group made up of nits?
The Lice Girls!

You're so dumb, you think the English Channel is a British TV station.

Why do dinosaurs wear glasses?
So they don't step on other dinosaurs.

What's the difference between a marshmallow and a pykost?
What's a pykost?
About two dollars.

Boy: *'Grandpa, do you know how to croak?'*
Grandpa: *'No, I don't. Why?'*
Boy: *'Because Daddy says he'll be a rich man when you do!'*

Did you hear what Dumb Donald did when he offered to paint the garage for his dad?
The instructions said put on three coats – so he put on his jacket, his raincoat and his overcoat!

Why did the boy wear a life jacket in bed?
Because he slept on a waterbed.

Home economics teacher: *'Joe, what are the best things to put into a chocolate cake?'*
Joe: *'Teeth!'*

Handsome Harry: *'Every time I walk past a girl, she sighs.'*
Wisecracking William: *'With relief!'*

Did you hear about the girl who was so keen on road safety that she always wore white at night?
Last winter she was knocked down by a snow plough.

What does a fool pour over his meat?
Thick gravy.

What do you call a red-headed fool?
A ginger nut.

Did you hear about my brother?
He saw a moose's head hanging on a wall and went into the next room to find the rest of it!

Why did the lion feel sick after he'd eaten the priest?
Because it's hard to keep a good man down.

You're so dumb, when you went to the mind reader they couldn't find anything to read.

'Mum,' Richard yelled from the kitchen. 'You know that dish you were always worried I'd break?'

'Yes dear, what about it?' said his mum.

'Well . . . your worries are over.'

Did you hear about the boy who wanted to run away to the circus?

He ended up in a flea circus!

What do young female monsters do at parties?

They go around looking for edible bachelors!

Why did Silly Sue throw her guitar away?

Because it had a hole in the middle.

Little Susie stood in the department store near the escalator, watching the moving handrail.

'Something wrong, little girl?' asked the security guard.

'Nope,' replied Susie. 'I'm just waiting for my chewing gum to come back.'

Dad, can you write in the dark?

I suppose so.

Good. Can you sign my report card, please?

Jane: *'Do you like me?'*

Wayne: *'As girls go, you're fine . . . and the sooner you go, the better!'*

First witch: *'I took my son to the zoo yesterday.'*

Second witch: *'Really? Did they keep him?'*

Did you hear about the fool who got a boomerang for his birthday?

He spent the next two days trying to throw the old one away.

A boy was staying in an old house, and in the middle of the night, he meets a ghost.

'I've been walking these corridors for 300 years,' said the ghost.

'In that case, can you tell me where the bathroom is?' asked the boy.

RIDDLE ME ONCE

What's the difference between a joke and a wise guy?
One is funny, and one thinks he's funny.

If a butcher is two metres tall and has size 11 feet, what does he weigh?
Meat.

What are two things you cannot have for breakfast?
Lunch and dinner.

What's the last thing you take off before bed?
Your feet off the floor.

Who gets the sack every time he goes to work?
The postman.

What dance do hippies hate?
A square dance.

What part of a fish weighs the most?
The scales.

Why don't bananas get lonely?
Because they hang around in bunches.

How long should a person's legs be?
Long enough to reach their feet.

Can a snail have houseguests?

Three men were in a boat. It capsized, but only two got their hair wet. Why?
The third man was bald!

What do you call a pretty and friendly witch?
A failure.

What can you serve, but never eat?
A tennis ball.

What did the piece of wood say to the drill?
You bore me.

What has ears but cannot hear?
A field of corn.

What is the difference between a hungry person and a greedy person?
One longs to eat, and the other eats too long.

Can a match box?
No, but a tin can!

Is it easier to break the long jump world record in a leap year?

When a boy falls into the water, what is the first thing he does?
Gets wet.

Why did the boy laugh after his operation?
Because the doctor put him in stitches.

What is bigger when it's upside down?
The number 6.

What's green and pecks on trees?
Woody Wood Pickle.

What's big and white and can't jump over a fence?
A fridge.

What ten letter word starts with fuel?
A-U-T-O-M-O-B-I-L-E.

If olive oil is made from olives and peanut oil is made from peanuts, what is baby oil made from?

_____

What can you give away but also keep?
A cold.

_____

What starts working when it's fired?
A rocket.

_____

What has eyes but cannot see?
A potato.

_____

What is put on a table and cut but never eaten?
A pack of cards.

_____

Which word if pronounced right is wrong and if pronounced wrong is right?
Wrong.

_____

Which king was purple and had many wives?
King Henry the Grape.

Does a death adder die if it bites its own tongue?

_____

Why is a bride always out of luck on her wedding day?
Because she never marries the best man.

_____

What is the best cure for dandruff?
Baldness.

_____

What goes in many different colours but always comes out blue?
A swimmer on a cold day!

_____

What are feathers good for?
Birds.

_____

Why did the boy throw butter out the window?
Because he wanted to see a butterfly!

When things go wrong what can you always count on?
Your fingers.

Where does Friday come before Wednesday?
In the dictionary.

What do ghosts use to type letters?
A type-frighter.

What has eyes that cannot see, a tongue that cannot taste, and a soul that cannot die?
A shoe.

What race is never run?
A swimming race.

Why are elephants wrinkled all over?
Because they can't fit on an ironing board.

What do you call a man who shaves fifteen times a day?
A barber.

What do well-behaved young lambs say to their mothers?
Thank ewe!

What has no legs but can walk?
A pair of shoes.

What's the difference between dinosaurs and dragons?
Dinosaurs are still too young to smoke.

What does a girl look for but hopes she'll never find?
A hole in her pantyhose.

What trees do fortune tellers prefer?
Palms.

What clothes does a house wear?
Address.

What kind of dress can never be worn?
Your address.

Why is an island like the letter T?
Because it's in the middle of water.

Why did the boy put his bed in the fireplace?
So he could sleep like a log.

If everyone bought a white car, what would we have?
A white carnation.

How many apples can you put in an empty box?
One. After that it's not empty anymore.

What is at the end of the world?
The letter 'D'.

What is the longest word in the world?
Smiles, because there is a mile between the beginning and the end.

What's green and wiggly and goes 'hith'?
A snake with a lisp.

Why did the cyclops give up teaching?
Because he only had one pupil.

The more you take, the more you leave behind. What am I?
Footsteps.

What gets wet the more you dry?
A towel!

What did Cinderella say when her photos weren't ready?
Some day my prints will come.

When is a bird not a bird?
When it's aloft.

What did Tennessee?
The same thing Arkansas.

What runs across the floor without legs?
Water.

What breaks when you say it?
Silence!

What is a prickly pear?
Two hedgehogs.

What's taken before you get it?
Your picture.

What is big, red and eats rocks?
A big red rock eater.

What's the centre of gravity?
The letter 'V'.

When is a chair like a woman's dress?
When it's satin.

HEDGEHOGS IN LOVE

Obviously radical babies

Why do we dress baby girls in pink and baby boys in blue?
Because babies can't dress themselves.

What does every winner lose in a race?
Their breath.

When the man was run over by a steamroller, what was proved?
That he had lots of guts.

What runs but doesn't get anywhere?
A refrigerator!

What bet can never be won?
The alphabet.

If nothing ever sticks to Teflon, how does Teflon stick to the pan?

What burns longer, a 10 centimetre candle or a 20 centimetre candle?
Neither, they both burn shorter.

When will water stop flowing downhill?
When it reaches the bottom.

Why do firemen wear red suspenders?
To keep their trousers up.

What is always coming but never arrives?
Tomorrow.

What's a vampire's favourite dog?
A bloodhound!

What's the difference between an oak tree and a tight shoe?
One makes acorns, the other makes corns ache.

I should have bought a larger size... These shoes are making my acorns ache!

HOW MANY . . . ?

How many soccer players does it take to change a light bulb?
Eleven, one to change it, the others to jump about, hugging and kissing him.

How many kite fliers does it take to change a light bulb?
Ten, one to change it and the other nine to blow as hard as they can to get a wind going.

How many aerobics teachers does it take to change a light bulb?
Five, one to change it, the others to say, 'A little to the left, a little to the right, a little to the left, a little to the right.'

One.
How many psychics does it take to change a light bulb?

How many roadies does it take to change a light bulb?
One two, one two, one two.

How many fire officers does it take to change a light bulb?
Four, one to change it, the others to stand by with a hose.

Why didn't the foolish goalkeeper catch the ball?
He thought that's what the net was for.

How many punk rockers does it take to change a light bulb?
Two, one to change it and the other to smash the old one on his forehead.

How many cave men does it take to change a light bulb?
What light bulbs?

How many astronomers does it take to change a light bulb?
None, they prefer the dark.

How many country music singers does it take to change a light bulb?
Two, one to change it, the other to sing about how heartbroken he is that the old one is finished.

How many accountants does it take to change a light bulb?
Sorry, there's no money left in the budget for another light bulb.

How many surgeons does it take to change a light bulb?
One, but only when a donor bulb is available.

How many robots does it take to change a light bulb?
One, but it needs 500 humans to have programmed it correctly.

How many models does it take to change a light bulb?
None, they don't want to ruin their nails.

How many taxi drivers does it take to change a light bulb?
None, they won't even change a $5 note.

How many executives does it take to change a light bulb?
'First we have to hold a series of meetings to discuss the issue.'

How many lawyers does it take to change a light bulb?
Three, one to sue the power company, one to sue the electrician who wired the house, and one to sue the bulb manufacturers.

How many actors does it take to change a light bulb?
Two, one to change it, the other to criticise his performance.

How many cheapskates does it take to change a light bulb?
None, they'd prefer to sit in the dark.

How many skunks does it take to change a light bulb?
A phew.

How many road workers does it take to change a light bulb?
Seven, one to change it, five to stand around leaning on their shovels and one to go and fetch lunch for them all.

How many baseball players does it take to change a light bulb?

Two, one to change it, the other to signal which way to do it.

How many movie directors does it take to change a light bulb?

One, but he wants it done over and over again until he's perfectly happy.

How many Santa Claus does it take to change a light bulb?

None, because there is no Santa Claus.

How many safety inspectors does it take to change a light bulb?

Ten, one to change it and nine to hold the ladder.

How many gardeners does it take to change a light bulb?

It depends whether it's the right season to change bulbs.

How many hamsters does it take to change a light bulb?

Don't be silly, how would a hamster get up to a light bulb.

How many elephants does it take to change a light bulb?

Two, but it has to be a pretty big light bulb!

How many waiters does it take to change a light bulb?

None, not even a blown globe can catch a waiter's eye.

How many teachers does it take to change a light bulb?

None, they leave it to their students as an exercise.

How many circus performers does it take to change a light bulb?
Five, one to change it, the others to hold the net.

How many philosophers does it take to change a light bulb?
Well, that's a very interesting question.

How many tourists does it take to change a light bulb?
Ten, one to change it and the other nine to take photos.

How many magicians does it take to change a light bulb?
What do you want it changed into?

There's always one in every crowd. Someone willing to try on the HEY Look trick in the middle of a juggling act.

How many jugglers does it take to change a light bulb?
Just one, but they need three light bulbs.

How many fishermen does it take to change a light bulb?
Ten, one to change it, the others to argue about how big it is.

How many clothing shop assistants does it take to change a light bulb?
Three, one to change it, one to say how well it fits and one to say that the colour is perfect.

How many siblings does it take to change a light bulb?
It's your turn, I did it last time.
No you didn't, I did.
I did.
I did.

DOCTOR, DOCTOR

Doctor, Doctor, I have a carrot growing out of my ear.

Amazing! How could that have happened?

I don't understand it. I planted cabbages in there!

Doctor, Doctor, I've got wind!
Can you give me something?

Yes – here's a kite!

Doctor, Doctor, I feel like a spoon!

Well, sit down and don't stir!

Doctor, Doctor, can I have a bottle of aspirin and a pot of glue?

Why?

Because I've got a splitting headache!

Doctor, Doctor, how was my check-up?

Perfect. You'll live to be 80.

But I am 80.

In that case, it's been nice knowing you.

Doctor, Doctor, I came as quick as I could. What's the problem?

Your lab results are back and you've only got 24 hours to live.

That's terrible.

There's worse. I've been trying to call you since yesterday.

Doctor, Doctor, can I have a second opinion?

Of course, come back tomorrow.

Doctor, Doctor, I have a hoarse throat.

The resemblance doesn't end there.

Doctor, Doctor, what's good for biting fingernails?
Very sharp teeth.

Doctor, Doctor, will this ointment clear up my spots?
I never make rash promises!

Doctor, Doctor, sometimes I feel like an onion and sometimes I feel like a cucumber.
You've got yourself in a bit of a pickle.

Doctor, Doctor, my wife's contractions are only five minutes apart.
Is this her first child?
No, this is her husband.

Doctor, Doctor, I feel like a bee.
Buzz off. I'm busy!

Doctor, Doctor, you have to help me out!
That's easily done, which way did you come in?

Doctor, Doctor, I keep thinking I'm a dog.
Sit on the couch and we'll talk about it.
But I'm not allowed on the furniture!

Doctor, Doctor, my baby looks just like his father.

Never mind – just as long as he's healthy.

Doctor, Doctor, I feel like a needle.

I see your point!

Doctor, Doctor, I think I need glasses.

You certainly do – you've just walked into a restaurant!

Doctor, Doctor, I keep thinking there's two of me.

One at a time please!

Doctor, Doctor, I've got a terrible cold. What should I do?

Go home, take a hot bath then stand outside in the cold with no clothes on.

But if I do that, I'll get pneumonia.

That's the idea. I can treat pneumonia. I can't treat a cold.

Doctor, Doctor, I think I'm suffering from déjà vu.

Haven't I seen you before?

Doctor, Doctor, I'm suffering from hallucinations.

I'm sure you are only imagining it.

Doctor, Doctor, I think I'm a python.

You can't get around me that easily, you know!

Doctor, Doctor, I think I'm a computer.
How long have you felt like this?
Ever since I was switched on!

Doctor, Doctor, I don't think I'm a computer anymore.
Now I think I'm a desk.
You're just letting things get on top of you.

Doctor, Doctor, I think I'm a snail.
Don't worry. We'll soon have you out of your shell.

Doctor, Doctor, I need something for my temper.
Just wait 'til you get the bill.

Doctor, Doctor, I ate some oysters and now I'm feeling sick.
Were they fresh?
How can you tell?
You open the shell and have a look.
You're not supposed to eat the shell?

Doctor, Doctor, some days I feel like a teepee and other days I feel like a wigwam.
Relax, you're two tents!

Doctor, Doctor, I've spent so long at my computer that I now see double.
Well, walk around with one eye shut.

Doctor, Doctor, I feel like a racehorse.
Take one of these every four laps!

Why do doctors wear masks?
Because if they make a mistake no-one will know who did it!

Doctor, Doctor, I'm a wrestler and I feel awful.
Get a grip on yourself then.

Doctor, Doctor, I think I'm a rubber band.
Why don't you stretch yourself out on the couch there, and tell me all about it?

Doctor, Doctor, I'm having trouble with my breathing.
I'll give you something that will soon put a stop to that!

Doctor, Doctor, I have yellow teeth, what should I do?
Wear a brown tie.

Doctor, Doctor, I feel like a strawberry.
I can see you're in a bit of a jam.

Doctor, Doctor, sometimes I think I'm a biscuit.
You're crackers.

Doctor, Doctor, I keep thinking I'm a billiard ball.
Well, get back to the cue.

Doctor, Doctor, I'm so ugly what can I do about it?
Hire yourself out for Halloween parties.

Doctor, Doctor, I feel like a pair of curtains.
Oh, pull yourself together!

Doctor, Doctor, what is the best way to avoid biting insects?
Don't bite any.

Doctor, Doctor, I feel like a sheep.
That's baaaaaaaaaad!

Doctor, Doctor, have you taken my temperature?
No. Is it missing?

Doctor, Doctor, I've been turned into a hare!
Stop rabbiting on about it.

Doctor, Doctor, tell me straight. Is it bad?
Just don't start watching any new TV shows.

Doctor, Doctor, if I give up wine, women and song, will I live longer?
No, but it will seem longer.

Doctor, Doctor, I feel like a pair of socks.
Well I'll be darned.

Doctor, Doctor, I'm at death's door.
Don't worry, I'll pull you through.

Doctor, Doctor, you've got to help me
I keep thinking I'm a bridge.
What's come over you?
So far, a truck, a motorcycle and
two cars.

Doctor, Doctor, I feel like I'm part of
the Internet!
Well you do look a site.

Doctor, Doctor, everyone keeps
throwing me in the garbage.
Don't talk rubbish!

Doctor, Doctor, I've got jelly in my ear.
You're just a trifle deaf.

Doctor, Doctor, I feel like an apple.
Well don't worry, I won't bite.

Doctor, Doctor, I think I'm turning into
a woman.
Well, you are 16 now Amanda.

Doctor, Doctor, should I surf the
Internet on an empty stomach?
No, you should do it on a computer.

Doctor, Doctor, I think I've been bitten by a vampire.
Drink this glass of water.
Will it make me better?
No, but I'll be able to see if your neck leaks!

Doctor Doctor, I keep hearing a ringing in my ears.
Where else did you expect to hear it?

Doctor, Doctor, I'm boiling up!
Just simmer down!

Doctor Doctor, I keep thinking I'm a fruitcake.
What's got into you?
Flour, raisins and cherries.

Doctor, Doctor, I've just swallowed a pen.
Well sit down and write your name!

Doctor, Doctor, when I press with my finger here . . . it hurts, and here . . . it hurts, and here . . . and here!
What do you think is wrong with me?
Your finger's broken!

A GUARANTEED CURE FOR SLEEPWALKING

Doctor, Doctor, how can I cure my sleepwalking?
Sprinkle tacks on your bedroom floor!

Doctor, Doctor, will I be able to play the violin when my hand heals?
Of course.
Great. Because I couldn't play it before.

Doctor, Doctor, I think I'm a clock.
You're winding me up.

Doctor, Doctor, I'm a burglar!
Have you taken anything for it?

Doctor, Doctor, I keep thinking I'm a spider.
What a web of lies!

Doctor, Doctor, everyone hates me.
Don't be silly, not everyone has met you yet.

Doctor, Doctor, I keep thinking I'm a doorknob.
Now don't fly off the handle.

Doctor, Doctor, I think I'm a moth.
So why did you come around then?
Well, I saw this light at the window . . .

Doctor, Doctor, I feel like a bird.
I'll tweet you in a minute.

Doctor, Doctor, you've taken out my tonsils, my appendix, my gall bladder and one of my kidneys but I still feel sick.
That's enough out of you.

Doctor, Doctor, I think I'm a calculator.
Great, can you help me with my accounts please?

Doctor, Doctor, everyone thinks I'm a liar.
Well, that's hard to believe!

Doctor, Doctor, I feel like a tennis racket.
You must be too highly strung.

Doctor, Doctor, I keep painting myself gold.
Don't worry, it's just a gilt complex.

Doctor, Doctor, I feel like a dog.
Sit!

Doctor, Doctor, sometimes I think there are two of me.
Good, you can pay both bills on the way out.

What did one tonsil say to the other tonsil?
Get dressed up, the doctor is taking us out!

Doctor, Doctor, I keep seeing an insect spinning.
Don't worry. It's just a bug that's going around.

Doctor, Doctor, I keep thinking I'm a yo-yo.
How are you feeling?
Oh, up and down.

Doctor, Doctor . . . My son swallowed a pen, what should I do?
Use a pencil instead!

Doctor, Doctor, what's wrong with me?
Well, you've got a carrot up your nose, a bean in one ear and a French fry in the other. I'd say you're not eating properly.

Doctor, Doctor, my hands won't stop shaking.
Do you drink a lot?
No, most of it spills.

Doctor, Doctor, I swallowed a whole cantaloupe.
You're just feeling melon-choly.

Doctor, Doctor, I keep thinking I'm a mosquito.
Go away, sucker!

Doctor, Doctor, my stomach is sore.
Stop your belly-aching.

Doctor, Doctor, I think I'm an electric eel.
That's shocking!

Doctor, Doctor, people keep disagreeing with me.
No they don't.

Doctor, Doctor, I think I'm a caterpillar.
Don't worry. You'll soon change.

Doctor, Doctor, how long have I got?
10.
10 what? 10 months? 10 weeks?
10, 9, 8, 7 …

Doctor, Doctor, my hands are killing me.
Take them off your throat.

Doctor, Doctor, I keep seeing double.
Please sit on the couch.
Which one?

Doctor, Doctor, I keep stealing things.
Take one of these pills and if that doesn't work, bring me back a computer.

Doctor, Doctor, I need some acetylsalicylic acid.
You mean aspirin?
That's it. I can never remember that word.

Doctor, Doctor, my nose is running.
You'd better tie it up then.

Doctor, Doctor, I keep thinking I'm a computer.
My goodness, you'd better come to my surgery right away!
I can't, my power cable won't reach that far!

Doctor, Doctor, I think I'm a frog.
What's wrong with that?
I think I'm going to croak!

Even as a child ... Bernard was always different from the other kids.

Doctor, Doctor, sometimes I feel like a goat.

How long has this been going on?

Ever since I was a kid.

Doctor, Doctor, I think I'm a snake, about to shed its skin.

Why don't you go behind the screen and slip into something more comfortable, then!

Doctor, Doctor, my little boy has just swallowed a roll of film.

Hmmm. Let's hope nothing develops!

Doctor, Doctor, how can I stop my nose from running?

Stick your foot out and trip it up!

Doctor, Doctor, my sister thinks she's a lift.

Well tell her to come in.

I can't, she doesn't stop at this floor!

Doctor, Doctor, I think I'm a nit.

Will you get out of my hair?

Doctor, Doctor, my hair keeps falling out. Can you give me something to keep it in?

Sure, here's a paper bag.

Doctor, Doctor, I keep seeing spots.

Have you seen an optometrist?

No, just spots.

Doctor. I keep seeing spots!

I think you need to see an Optometrist. A friend of mine is an Optometrist...I can get you a good deal

Doctor, Doctor, my sister keeps thinking she's invisible.
Which sister?

Doctor, Doctor, will you treat me?
No you'll have to pay like everybody else.

Doctor, doctor, since the operation on my leg, I lean one way.
I think you're all right.

Doctor, Doctor, my baby's swallowed some explosives.
Well don't annoy him. We don't want him to go off.

Doctor, Doctor, I feel like a window.
Where's the pane?

Doctor, Doctor, I feel like a dog!
Then go see a vet!

Doctor, Doctor, I keep thinking I'm a donut.
Let's talk about this over coffee.

Doctor, Doctor, I keep thinking I'm a vampire.
Necks, please!

Doctor, Doctor, I feel like a pack of cards.
I'll deal with you later!

Doctor, Doctor, I've swallowed my harmonica!
Well, it's a good thing you don't play the piano.

45

Doctor, Doctor, I keep thinking I'm a joke.
Don't make me laugh.

Doctor, Doctor, I've got gas! Can you give me something?
Yes! Here's my car.

Doctor, Doctor, I swallowed a bone.
Are you choking?
No, I really did!

Doctor, Doctor, I keep thinking I'm a $10 note.
Go shopping, the change will do you good.

Doctor, Doctor, this ointment you gave me makes my arm smart!
Try putting some on your head.

Doctor, Doctor, I keep thinking I'm God.
When did this start?
After I created the sun, then the earth . . .

Doctor, Doctor, my little brother thinks he's a computer.
Well, bring him in so I can cure him.
I can't. I need to use him to finish my homework!

Doctor, Doctor, every time I stand up I see visions of Mickey Mouse and Pluto and every time I sit down I see Donald Duck!

How long have you been having these Disney spells?

Doctor, Doctor, these pills you gave me for BO . . .

What's wrong with them?

They keep slipping out from under my arms!

Doctor, Doctor, I can't get to sleep.

Sit on the edge of the bed and you'll soon drop off.

Doctor, Doctor, I snore so loud that I keep myself awake.

Sleep in another room, then.

Doctor, Doctor, I'm becoming invisible.

Yes, I can see you're not all there!

Doctor, Doctor, I keep seeing green aliens with two heads and four legs.

Have you seen a psychiatrist?

No, just green aliens with two heads and four legs.

Doctor, Doctor, I think I might croak.

It's just a frog in your throat.

Doctor, Doctor, the first thirty minutes I'm up every morning I feel dizzy, what should I do?
Get up half an hour later.

Doctor, Doctor, I can't feel my legs.
That's because we had to amputate your arms.

Doctor, doctor, have you got something for a migraine?
Take this hammer and hit yourself on the head.

Doctor, Doctor, what did the X-ray of my head show?
Absolutely nothing!

Doctor, Doctor, I've lost all my hair.
That's a bald statement.

Doctor, Doctor, everyone keeps ignoring me.
Next please!

Doctor, Doctor, I've broken my arm in two places.
Well, don't go back there again.

Doctor, Doctor, I dream there are zombies under my bed. What can I do?
Saw the legs off your bed.

Doctor, Doctor, I think I'm a butterfly.
Will you say what you mean and stop flitting about!

Doctor, Doctor, I have a ringing in my ears!
Well, answer it.

Doctor, Doctor, I've a split personality.
Well, you'd better both sit down, then.

Doctor, Doctor, my leg hurts, what can I do?
Limp.

Doctor, Doctor . . . did you hear about the boy who swallowed some money?
No? Well, there's no change yet!

Doctor, Doctor, I think I'm a drill.
How boring for you!

Doctor, Doctor, I feel like an apple.
We must get to the core of this!

Doctor, Doctor, my husband smells like a fish.
Poor sole!

Doctor, Doctor, I accidentally ate my pillow.
Don't be so down in the mouth.

Doctor, Doctor, my girlfriend thinks she's a duck.
You'd better bring her in to see me right away.
I can't. She's already flown south for the winter.

Doctor, Doctor, I think I'm a moth.
Get out of the way. You're in my light!

You say your husband smells like a fish? That's because he _is_ a fish!

Doctor, Doctor, I feel run down.
You should be more careful crossing the road then.

Doctor, Doctor, I'm afraid of the dark.
Then leave the light on.

Doctor, Doctor, I swallowed a spoon.
Well, try to relax and don't stir.

Doctor Doctor, I feel like a bell.
Well take these and if they don't work, give me a ring.

Doctor, Doctor, my sister thinks she's a squirrel!
Sounds like a nut case to me!

Doctor, Doctor, something is preying on my mind!
Don't worry, it will probably starve to death.

Why did the doctor tiptoe past the medicine cabinet?

Because she didn't want to wake the sleeping pills!

Doctor, Doctor, I dreamed that I ate a large marshmallow!
Did you wake up without a pillow?

Doctor, Doctor, I think I'm a DVD.
I thought I'd seen you before.

Doctor, Doctor, my son swallowed my razor-blade.
Well, just use your electric razor.

Doctor, Doctor, I keep thinking I'm a fish.
You've got water on the brain.

Doctor, Doctor, I think I'm losing my mind.
Don't worry, you won't miss it.

Doctor, Doctor, I have a pain in the eye every time I drink hot chocolate!
Take the spoon out of your mug before you drink.

Doctor, Doctor, I think I'm a woodworm.
How boring for you!

Doctor, Doctor, I think I'm a yo-yo.
You're stringing me along!

When do doctors get angry?
When they run out of patience (patients).

Doctor, Doctor, I only have 59 seconds to live!
Just a minute!

Doctor, doctor, should I file my nails?
No, throw them away like everyone else does.

Doctor, Doctor, I feel like a piano.
Wait a moment while I make some notes.

Doctor, Doctor, my wooden leg is giving me a lot of pain.
Why's that?
My wife keeps hitting me over the head with it!

Doctor, Doctor, I'm turning into a trash can.
Don't talk such rubbish.

Doctor, Doctor, my eyesight is getting worse.
You're absolutely right, this is a post office.

Doctor, Doctor, I've lost my memory.
When did this happen?
When did what happen?

Doctor, Doctor, I think I'm getting shorter!
You'll just have to be a little patient.

Doctor, Doctor, it hurts when I do this!
Well, don't do that.

What do you call a surgeon with eight arms?
A doctopus.

WHAT DO YOU CALL ... ?

What do you call a man with a paper bag on his head?
Russell!

What do you call a dinosaur that never gives up?
A try and try and try-ceratops.

What do you call an old and foolish vampire?
A silly old sucker!

What do you call a man with a car on his head?
Jack!

What do you call a man with a rug on his head?
Matt.

What do you call a man with rabbits in his trousers?
Warren.

What do you call a robot who takes the longest route?
R2 Detour!

What do you call a man with a bus on his head?
Dead.

What do you call a cat that plays football?
Puss in boots.

What do you call a girl with a tennis racket on her head?
Annette!

People have told me my wig looks like a rug... But I won't have a word of it!

To me it looks more like a mat!

What do you call a flying policeman?
Heli-copper!

What do you call an overweight E.T.?
An extra cholesterol.

What do you call a woodpecker with no beak?
A headbanger.

What do you call an unmarried female moth?
Myth.

What do you call a Russian gardener?
Ivanhoe.

What do you call a man with beef, gravy and vegetables on his head?
Stu.

What do you call a girl with a frog on her head?
Lily!

What do you call a healthy insect?
A Vitamin Bee.

What do you call a man who is always around when you need him?
Andy.

What do you call a woman with a Christmas tree on her head?
Carol.

What do you call a man with a Christmas tree on his head?
Noel.

What do you call a pig with no clothes on?
Streaky bacon.

What do you call cattle that always sit down?
Ground beef.

What do you call a woman with one foot on each side of a river?
Bridget.

What will Bob the Builder be called when he retires?
Bob.

What do you call a fairy who never takes a bath?
Stinkerbell!

What do you call an elephant that flies?
A jumbo jet.

The new season's windswept look

What do you call a woman standing in a breeze?
Gail!

What do you call an egg laid by a dog?
A pooched egg!

What do you call a camel with three humps?
Humphrey.

What do you call a camel with no humps?
A horse.

It always amazes me how those JUMBO JETS stay in the air!

UURRRRRRRR
Flaps up...check...engines to speed...
...clear for take off!

What do you call the ghost of a chicken?
A poultrygeist.

What do you call a sleeping bull?
A bulldozer!

What do you call a protest march by devils?
A demon-stration.

What do you call a man with a large black and blue mark on his head?
Bruce!

What do you call a man who likes to work out?
Jim!

What do you call a woman in the distance?
Dot!

What do you call a boy hanging on the wall?
Art!

What do you call a cat who wins a fight?
Claudia.

What do you call a chicken that lays light bulbs?
A battery hen.

What do you call a witch without a broomstick?
A witch-hiker.

What do you call a woman with a cat on her head?
Kitty!

What do you call a man with a seagull on his head?
Cliff!

What do you call a carrot who talks back to the cook?
A fresh vegetable!

What do you call two rows of vegetables?
A dual cabbageway.

What do you call woman with a radiator on her head?
Anita.

What do you call a German barber?
Herr Dresser.

What do you call a man floating in the sea?
Bob.

What do you call a duck with fangs?
Count Quackula.

What do you call an elephant that never washes?
A smellyphant.

What do you call a frog with no legs?
Unhoppy.

What do you call a man with a map on his head?
Miles!

What do you call a man who drives a truck?
Laurie.

What do you call a mouse that can pick on a monster?
Sir.

What do you call the autobiography of a shark?
A fishy story.

What do you call a woman who can balance a bottle of beer on her head?
Beatrix.

What do you call a skunk in a courthouse?
Odour in the court!

What do you call a man who had an accident?
Derek!

What do you call a lady standing in the middle of a tennis court?
Annette!

What do you call a man with a spade?
Doug!

What do you call a man without a spade?
Douglas!

What do you call a woman with one leg?
Eileen!

What do you call a flea who flies inside a fool's head?
A space invader.

What do you call the chief's daughter when she's in trouble?
Miss Chief!

What do you call a boy with an encyclopedia in his pants?
Smarty pants.

What do you call a monkey with a banana in each ear?
Anything, he can't hear you.

What do you call a snake that works for the government?
A civil serpent.

What do you call a skeleton who sits around doing nothing?
Lazy bones.

What do you call a monster who comes to collect your laundry?
An undie-taker.

What do you call a man with some cat scratches on his head?
Claude!

What do you call a woman who gambles?
Betty.

What do you call a man sitting in a tree?
Woody.

What do you call a train full of gum?
A chew chew train!

What do you call a cat that joined the Red Cross?
A first aid kit!

What do you call a man with a truck on his head?
Deceased!

What do you call a bear with no fur?
A bare.

What do you call two witches who share a room?
Broom mates!

What do you call a man who owes money?
Bill!

What do you call a lion wearing a hat?
A dandy lion.

What do you call a woman with a tortoise on her head?
Shelley!

What do you call a woman who climbs up walls?
Ivy.

What do you call a man in a pile of leaves?
Russell!

What do you call a rabbit locked in a sauna?
A hot cross bunny!

What do you call a bee that buzzes quietly?
A mumble bee.

Master Hog demonstrating his famous... Pork Chop.

AAAARR-YA

What do you call a pig that does karate?
Pork chop.

What do you call a man with a legal document?
Will!

What do you call an elephant that flies straight up?
An elecopter.

What do you call a woman with a toilet on her head?
Lu!

What do you call a woman with two toilets on her head?
Lulu!

What do you call a hairy beast in a river?
A weir-wolf.

What do you call a young goat who visits a psychiatrist?
A mixed-up kid.

Well Doc... It was like this. It all started when I was a kid. I started acting like a goat... then I was hooked!

What do you call a well-behaved goose?
A propaganda.

What do you call someone who doesn't have all their fingers on one hand?
Normal. You have fingers on both hands!

What do you call a neurotic octopus?
A crazy, mixed-up squid.

What do you call someone who greets you at the school door every morning?
Matt.

What do you call an animal that drops from the clouds?
A reindeer.

What do you call two pigs who write letters to each other?
Pen-pals.

What do you call an arctic cow's house?
An igmoo.

What do you call a cow that eats grass?
A lawn mooer.

What do you call a detective skeleton?
Sherlock Bones.

What do you call a mosquito that prefers walking to flying?
An itch-hiker.

What do you call a penguin in the desert?
Lost.

What do you call a man with a plank on his head?
Edward!

What do you call a Russian fish?
A Tsardine.

What do you call a zebra without stripes?
A horse.

What do you call a deer with only one eye?
No idea.

What do you call a deer with no legs and only one eye?
Still no idea.

What do you call a pig who enjoys jumping from a great height?
A stydiver.

What do you call a crazy spaceman?
An astronut!

What do you call a fish with no eyes?
Fsh.

What do you call a crate of ducks?
A box of quackers.

What do you call a bird that lives underground?
A mynah bird.

What do you call a sheep in a bikini?
Bra-bra black sheep.

What do you call a fly when it retires?
A flew.

What do you call a messy cat?
Kitty litter.

REQUIRED READING

How to be Taller by Stan Dupp

Quick Snacks by Roland Butter

Speaking French by Lorna Lang Wedge

Can't Sleep at Night by Constance Snoarer

Wildcats in Sweden by Bjorn Free

My Holiday with the Penguins by Anne Tarctic

My Golden Wedding by Annie Versary

The Antarctic Ocean by IC Waters

Chinese Lanterns by Eric Trician

The Modern Police Force by Iris Tew

Making Millions by Ivor Lott

Boo! by Terry Fied

The Chocolate Bar by Ken I Havesum

Fighting off Burglars by Al Sayshun

Confessions of a Thief by I Dunnit

My Life as a Jockey by Rhoda Horse

Housing Problem by Rufus Quick

Making the Most of Life by Maxie Mumm

The Big Bang by Dinah Mite

A Ghost in the Attic by Howie Wales

There's a Wizard at my Door by Wade Aminit

The Laser Weapon by Ray Gunn

Up the Amazon by P Rhana

Getting Your Homework Done by Mae B Tomorrow

Collecting Reptiles by Croc A Dile

Out for the Count by Esau Stars

The Garlic Eater by I Malone

Smashing Glass by Eva Stone

Modern Policing by UR Nicked

Strong Winds by Gail Forse

Modern Haircuts by Sean Head

A Terrible Nightmare by Gladys Over

Across the African Plains by Ann T Lope

Roof Repairs by Lee King

The Hurricane by Rufus Blownoff

Vegetable Gardening by Rosa Cabbages

Seasons Greetings by Mary Christmas

Within minutes... the day at the beach became a swim in the ocean....

Holiday on the Beach by Sandy Shaw

A Ghost in My House by Olive N Fear

Falling from a Height by Eileen Toofar

Buying Insurance by Justin Case

Egyptian Mummies by M Barmer

The Terrible Problem by Major Setback

Sahara Journey by Rhoda Camel

Famous People by Hugh Did-Watt

Rice Growing by Paddy Field

Keeping Warm at Night by Ida Down

Town Planning by Sir Veyor

Eclipse of the Sun by Ray Oflight

Maths for Beginners by Algy Brar

In the Cannibal's Cauldron by Mandy Ceased

The Arabian Cookbook by Sultan Vinegar

How to Keep Out a Vampire by Dora Steele

Hungry Dog by Nora Bone

The Omen by B Warned

The Haunted House by Hugo First

Grand Canyon Adventures by Rhoda Donkey

Sunday Service by Neil Downe

The Best Day Ever by Trudy Light

Repairing Old Clothes by Fred Bare

The Hungry Bear by Aida Lott

Swinging from the Trees by Bab Boone

The Long Sleep by Anna Sthetic

Creature from Another World by A Lee-En

Hosting a Party by Maude D Merrier

Pants Down by Lucy Lastic

The Japanese Way of Death by Harri Kirri

Making Weatherproof Clothes by Ranier Day

Adding Up by Juan and Juan

Winter Heating by Ray D Ater

Lost in the Desert by Diana Thirst

Escape from the Monster by Jess N Time

Hanging From a Cliff by Alf Hall

Carpet Fitting by Walter Wall

A Hole in the Bucket by Lee King

The Invisible Man by Peter Out

A Sting in the Tale by B Keeper

The Rag and Bone Trade By Orson Cart

The Lady Artist by Andrew Pictures

The Greediest Monster by Buster Gutt

Easy Money by Robyn Banks

Litter Collection by Phil D Basket

The Wrong Shoe by Titus Canbe

The Long Walk to School by Mr Bus

Jail Break by Freida Prizner

A Time for Witch Hunting by Mae B Layta

Dealing with Bullies by Howard U Lykett

Bird Watching by Jack Daw

Terrible Spells by B Witcher

Swimming the English Channel by Frances Neer

Don't Leave Without Me by Isa Coming

Monsters I Have Known by O Penjaw

The Mad Cat by Claud Boddy

The Leaky Tap by Constant Dripping

The Millionaire by Iva Fortune

Clairvoyance Made Easy by IC Spooks

The Rainforest by Teresa Green

When Shall We Meet Again? by Miles Apart

Winning the Lottery by Jack Potts

My Crystal Ball by CA Lot

Romantic Remembrance by Valentine Card

Bird Watching by Mac Caw

Robbers Who Got Away With It by Hugh Dunnit

Pig Breeding by Lena Bacon

Keep on Trying by Percy Vere

World Atlas by Joe Graffie

Camping in Iceland by IC Blast

Telephone Problems by Ron Number

Don't Wake the Baby by Elsie Cries

In the Summer by Clement Weather

The Sad Woman by Paul Aidy

Dangerous Germs by Mike Robes

The Ghost of a Witch by Eve L Spirit

Stormy Day by A Pauline Weather

The Unknown Author by Anne Onymous

Foaming at the Mouth by Dee Monic

The Strongman by Everhard Muscles

Aching Joints by Arthur Itis

Will He Win? by Betty Wont

Kidnapped! by Caesar Quick

Close Shaves by Ray Zerr

A Load of Old Rubbish by Stephan Nonsense

Crossing Roads Safely by Luke Bothways

Horror Stories by RU Scared

Great Eggspectations by
Charles Chickens

Improve Your Garden by Anita Lawn

A Bang on the Head by Esau Stars

Brides and Grooms by Marie Mee

A Call For Assistance
by Linda Hand

Explosives for Beginners
by Dinah Might

How to be Shorter by Neil Down

Making Enemies From Your Friends
by Olive Alone

The Bad Tempered Werewolf by
Claudia Armoff

Broken Window by Eva Brick

Whodunnit? by Ivor Clew

My Life Selling Houses by Con Allday

I Saw a Witch by Denise R Knockin

The Worst Day Ever by Trudy Zasta

Ghosts and Ghouls by
Sue Pernatural

Cheese and Salami Dishes by
Della Katessen

Pain and Sorrow by Anne Guish

Beginning Magic by Beatrix Star

The Vampire's Victim by E Drew Blood

Infectious Diseases by Willie Catchit

The Runaway Horse by Gay Topen

Always Late by Chester Minnit

Summer Bites by Amos Quito

Swallowing Dr Jekyll's Potion by Iris Keverything

Kung Fu for Beginners by Flora Mugga

The Worst Journey in the World by Helen Back

Ghost Stories by IM Scared

How to Feed Werewolves by Nora Legge

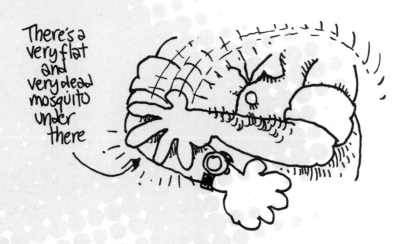

Reaching the Top by Ella Vator

Exercise At Home by Ben Dan Stretch

A Bullfighter's Life by Matt Adore

Christmas Traditions by Miss L Toe

The Broken Vase by Alex Plain

Garden Water Features by Lily Pond

Catching Criminals by Hans Upp

Hunting Witches by Count Miout

Igloo Building by Art Tick

Country Dancing by Hans Kneesanboomsadaisy

Witch in the Mirror by Douglas Cracked

Your Money or Your Life by Stan Den Deliver

How to Make Money by Robin Banks

Catching Crooks by Laura Norder

Poltergeist by Noi Zee Spirit

Classic Furniture by Ann Teaks

Never Challenge a Witch by Sheila Mazeya

Making Snacks by San Widge

Weekend Breaks by Gladys Friday

I Saw a Skeleton by Denise R Nobbly

83

FRENEMIES

Knock Knock. *Who's there?*
Jo! *Jo who?*
Jo jump in the lake!

They say that truth is stranger than fiction. And you're the proof.

Why do demons and ghouls get on so well?
Because demons are a ghoul's best friend.

Knock Knock. *Who's there?*
Alan! *Alan who?*
Alan a good cause!

Someone told me you're not fit to live with pigs but I stuck up for you and said you were.

You're so dumb, when your teacher said she wanted you to get ahead, she really meant 'a head'.

You're so ugly, when you enter a room, the mice jump on chairs.

I'd leave you with one thought if you had somewhere to put it.

Which of the witches' friends eats the fastest?
The goblin.

Knock Knock. *Who's there?*
Doris. *Doris who?*
The Doris locked so let me in.

Turn the other cheek. On second thoughts, don't. The view is just as ugly on that side.

You were so annoying on the airline flight that the steward told you to go and play outside.

You are as useless as a screen door on a submarine.

When is the cheapest time to phone friends?
When they're not home.

I'm not being rude, you're just being insignificant.

Your family is so poor, when the doorbell rings your sister has to shout out 'Ding, Dong.'

You're so ugly, the only dates you get are on a calendar.

Girl to friend: *'I'm sorry, I won't be able to come out tonight. I promised Dad I'd stay in and help him with my homework . . .'*

Go and sit down. Nobody can stand you.

You're so boring, you won't even talk to yourself.

What smells worse than a bad egg?
You do.

Why are giraffes good friends to have?
Because they stick their necks out for you.

'What shall we play today?' Tanya asked her best friend Emma.
'Let's play schools,' said Emma.
'Okay,' said Tanya. *'But I'm going to be absent.'*

You're such a bad cook, even the maggots go out for dinner.

If someone offered you a penny for your thoughts, they'd expect some change.

You're growing on me – like a wart.

86

Don't let your mind wander – it's too little to be let out alone.

Knock Knock. *Who's there?*
Hugo. *Hugo who?*
Hugo one way, I'll go the other.

How does a skeleton call his friends?
On a telebone.

With you here, your village must be missing its idiot.

This food isn't fit for a pig.
I'll get some for you that is then.

You have an open mind. Ideas just slip straight out.

I think a lot of people will go to his funeral.
Yes, to make sure he is dead.

Is it true your brother is an only child?

You're so dumb it takes you three hours to watch Sixty Minutes.

Your dog is so slow, he brings in last week's newspaper.

She'll lose her looks when she gets older, which just proves how lucky she is.

Do you notice how my voice fills the hall?

Yes, and did you notice how many people left to make way for it?

You're so ugly you have to trick or treat over the phone.

Jane was telling her friend about her holiday in Switzerland. Her friend asked, *'What did you think of the beautiful scenery?'*

'Oh, I couldn't see much,' said Jane. *'There were too many mountains in the way.'*

You're dark and handsome. When it's dark, you're handsome.

What is the difference between you and wild camel?

One is a big, smelly, bad-tempered beast and the other is an animal.

Knock Knock. *Who's there?*
Roxanne. *Roxanne who?*
Roxanne pebbles are all over your garden.

Mr Cannibal: *'I've brought a friend home for dinner.'*
Mrs Cannibal: *'But I've already made a stew.'*

Everyone has the right to be ugly, but you abused the privilege.

You would be out of your depth in a puddle.

Anyone who told you to be yourself couldn't have given you worse advice.

Do you still love nature, despite what it did to you?

As an outsider, what do you think of the human race?

You don't bore people with long speeches. You can bore them with a short speech.

How many teenage girls does it take to change a light bulb?
One, but she'll be on the phone for five hours telling all her friends about it.

If it's true that opposites attract, you'll meet someone who is good-looking, intelligent and cultured.

Knock Knock. *Who's there?*
Eliza. *Eliza who?*
Eliza wake at night thinking about you.

Knock Knock. *Who's there?*
Jim! *Jim who?*
Jim mind if we come in!

You're so dumb you stared at the orange juice container because it said 'Concentrate'.

Last time I saw someone as ugly as you, I had to pay admission.

Here's 50 cents. Call all your friends and bring me back the change.

Your feet are so smelly, your shoes refuse to come out of the closet.

The other shoes in the wardrobe could stand the smell no longer... so the stinky sandshoes were shown the door...

A BIT OF THIS . . .

What did the big chimney say to the little chimney?
You're too young to smoke.

How do you make a potato puff?
Chase it around the garden.

What's red and white?
Pink.

Are you awake?
No!

What is scared of wolves and swears?
Little Rude Riding Hood.

Two university professors are sitting on a verandah.
Professor 1: *'Have you read Marx?'*
Professor 2: *'Yes, these cane chairs will do it every time.'*

Why does the ocean roar?
You would too if you had crabs on your bottom.

Did I tell you the joke about the high wall?
I'd better not, you might not get over it.

What jam can't you eat?
A traffic jam!

How do fishermen make a net?
They make lots of holes and tie them together with string.

Why do mother kangaroos hate rainy days?
Because their kids have to play inside.

What's the difference between Santa Claus and a warm dog?
Santa wears the suit, but a dog just pants.

How do you clean the sky?
With a skyscraper.

What did the tie say to the hat?
You go on ahead, I'll just hang around.

Police officer: *'Can you please blow into this bag.'*
Motorist: *'Why, is your lunch too hot?'*

What's the definition of intense?
That's where campers sleep.

What can jump higher than a house?
Anything, houses can't jump!

What do you call a lazy toy?
An inaction figure.

What happened when the bell fell in the swimming pool?
It got wringing wet.

What did the ear 'ear?
Only the nose knows.

What's the hottest letter in the alphabet?
It's 'b', because it makes oil boil!

Why don't kangaroos ride bicycles?
Because they don't have thumbs to ring the little bell.

What is big and grey and out of bounds?
A tired kangaroo.

What's the difference between going to church and going to the movies?
At church, they say *'Stand up for Jesus.'* At the movies, they shout, *'Sit down for Christ's sake.'*

What do bees do if they need a ride?
Wait at a buzz stop.

What happened when there was a fight in the seafood restaurant?
Two fish got battered.

'Charley, why did Farley run through the screen door?' asked Mum. 'Because he wanted to strain himself!'

What did the shirt say to the blue jeans?
Meet you on the clothes line – that's where I hang out!

There are three kinds of people in the world. Those who can count. And those who can't.

Sheriff: *'You need a permit to catch fish.'*
Boy: *'What's wrong with worms?'*

Customer: *'Have you got William Shakespeare's* Hamlet?'
Bookshop owner: *'I don't know. When did he order it?'*

What did the big telephone say to the little telephone?
You're too young to get engaged.

Two prisoners escaped from custody. One was seven feet tall, the other four feet. Police searched high and low for them.

What's worse than finding a worm in your apple?
Finding half a worm!

What's green, covered in custard and sad?
Apple grumble.

Amy: *'Did you find your cat?'*
Karen: *'Yes, he was in the refrigerator.'*
Amy: *'Goodness, is he okay?'*
Karen: *'Yes, he's cool!'*

Can you lend me $1000?
I only have $800.
That's okay. You can owe me the other $200.

How do you make a Venetian blind?
Put a blindfold on him.

What's the difference between a young lady and a fresh loaf?
One is a well-bred maid and the other is well-made bread.

Why did the Mexican push his wife over the cliff?
Tequila.

What do you call a boomerang that doesn't come back to you?
A stick.

How do you make antifreeze?
Lock her outside in the cold.

What do you get when two prams collide?
A creche.

How do prisoners call home?
On cell phones.

How do tell which end of a worm is the head?
Tickle him in the middle and watch where he smiles.

What do you get when you cross a chicken and a caterpillar?
Drumsticks for everyone!

Where did the king keep his armies?
Up his sleevies.

Why did the farmer prepare his field with a steamroller?
He wanted to grow mashed potatoes.

What did the little light bulb say to its Mum?
I wuv you watts and watts.

How do you make a fire with two sticks?
Make sure one of them is a match.

What was more useful than the invention of the first telephone?
The second telephone.

Why was Thomas Edison able to invent the light bulb?
Because he was very bright.

What do you get if you cross a worm with a baby goat?
A dirty kid.

How do you get four suits for a couple of dollars?
Buy a pack of cards.

What wears nine gloves, eighteen shoes and a mask?
A baseball team.

What did the waterfall say to the fountain?
You're just a little squirt.

What do you get when you cross a duck with a rooster?
A bird that wakes you up at the quack of dawn!

What's the difference between a night watchman and a butcher?
One stays awake and the other weighs a steak!

What's brown and sounds like a bell?
Dung.

Why is six scared of seven?
Because 7-8-9.

What did the Pacific Ocean say to the Atlantic Ocean?
Nothing. It just waved.

What has a hundred legs but can't walk?
Fifty pairs of trousers.

What did the big hand of the clock say to the little hand?
Got a minute?

What do you do when you see two snails fighting?
Nothing, you just let them slug it out.

Knock, Knock. *Who's there?*
Gizza! *Gizza who?*
Gizza kiss!

What vegetable goes well with jacket potatoes?
Button mushrooms.

What did one ear say to the other ear?
Between you and me we need a haircut.

What's the difference between an elephant and a matterbaby?
What's a matterbaby?
Nothing, but thanks for asking!

When is a car like a frog?
When it is being toad.

What did one raindrop say to the other?
Two's company, three's a cloud.

What do you do if your nose goes on strike?
Picket.

Person 1: *'I've never been so insulted in all my life.'*

Person 2: *'You haven't been trying.'*

Where was Noah when the lights went out?
In d'ark.

We went for a holiday last year to a seaside town. It was so boring there that the tide went out one day and didn't come back!

Who's faster than a speeding bullet and full of food?
Super Market.

A house was burgled last night. Everything was stolen except for some soap and towels that were on top of a cupboard. Police are looking for some lowdown, dirty thieves.

What do you get when you cross a leopard with a watchdog?
A terrified postman.

Why did the bacteria cross the microscope?
To get to the other slide.

Statistics say that one in three people is a fool. So check your friends and if two of them seem okay, you're the one.

How did the rocket lose his job?
He was fired.

Where do you find giant snails?
At the ends of their fingers.

What did the pencil sharpener say to the pencil?
Stop going in circles and get to the point!

What do Alexander the Great and Kermit the Frog have in common?
The same middle name!

Why did the teacher wear dark glasses?
Because she had such a bright class.

A greyhound walks up to two horses at a bar.
Greyhound: *'Can I buy you both a drink?'*
The horses look at each other in amazement.
Horse 1: *'I didn't know dogs could talk.'*

A termite walks into a bar.
Termite: *'Is the bar tender tonight?'*

What do you get when you cross an elephant with a sparrow?
Broken telephone poles everywhere.

What do you get when you cross an orange with a squash court?
Orange squash.

A person pushes to the front of an airport queue: *'Excuse me, how long will the flight take?'*
Airline Official: *'Just a minute.'*
Person: *'Thank you.'*

Who invented the weekend?
Robinson Crusoe – he had his work done by Friday.

How much does Uluru (Ayers Rock) weigh?
One stone.

Where's your mum?
On holiday.
Jakarta?
No, she caught a plane.

So you are distantly related to the family next door, are you?
Yes. Their dog is our dog's brother.

Why was the glowworm unhappy?
Her children weren't very bright.

Where did Noah keep the bees?
In the ark hives.

I have ten legs, twenty arms and fifty-four feet. What am I?
A liar.

Which months have 28 days?
All of them.

What do you get when you cross a corgi with a clock?
A watchdog.

What do you get when you cross a Chinese leader with a cat?
Miaow Tse Tung.

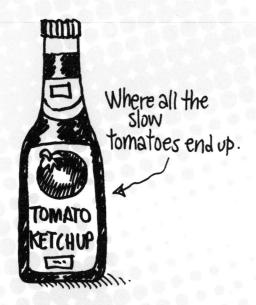

Where all the slow tomatoes end up.

What did one tomato say to the one behind him?
Ketchup!

What's the best way to win a race?
Run faster than everyone else.

What did the egg say to the whisk?
I know when I'm beaten.

What do you get if you cross a cowboy with a stew?
Hopalong Casserole.

What would you call superman if he lost all his powers?
Man.

Nervous passenger: *'Do these planes crash often?'*
Pilot: *'Only once.'*

How can you tell a dogwood tree?
By its bark.

What did the electrician's wife say when he got home?
Wire you insulate?

Where do old Volkswagens go?
To the old volks home.

Why did the koala fall out of the tree?
Because it was dead.

What time do most people go to the dentist?
Tooth-hurty.

Did you know that Davey Crockett had three ears?
A right ear, a left ear and a wild frontier.

What did the key say to the glue?
You wanna be in show biz kid?
Stick to me, I can open doors for you!

Duck: *'Do you have any lip gloss?'*
Storekeeper: *'Yes, of course. Will that be cash or credit?'*
Duck: *'Just put it on my bill.'*

What did the parents say to their son who wanted to play drums?
Beat it!

What sort of star is dangerous?
A shooting star.

What is the difference between a jeweller and a jailer?
A jeweller sells watches and a jailer watches cells!

Who was the smallest man in the world?
The guard that fell asleep on his watch.

Why did the traffic light turn red?
You would too if you had to change in the middle of the street!

When does the alphabet only have 24 letters?
When U and I aren't there.

Where did Captain Cook stand when he landed in Australia?
On his feet.

A horse walks into a bar.
Barman: *'Why the long face?'*

What did the power point say to the plug?
Socket to me.

What do all the Smiths in the telephone book have in common?
They all have telephones.

Dad, can you see a change in me?
No, why son?
Because I swallowed twenty cents.

What did the judge say to the dentist?
Do you swear to pull the tooth, the whole tooth and nothing but the tooth?

What's brown and sticky?
A stick.

Why was the maths book sad?
Because it had too many problems.

What's another word for tears?
Glumdrops.

Which bus sailed the oceans?
Columbus.

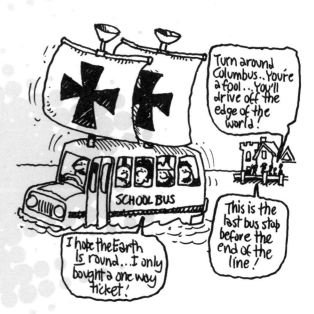

Did Adam and Eve have a date?
No, they had an apple.

What are government workers called in Spain?
Seville servants.

What's Chinese and deadly?
Chop sueycide.

What invention allows you to see through walls?
A window.

During which battle was Lord Nelson killed?
His last one.

When does B come after U?
When you take some of its honey!

Why was the butcher worried?
His job was at steak!

Why did the criminals whisper in the meadow?
Because they didn't want to be overheard by the grass.

What's big white and furry and found in outback Australia?
A very lost polar bear.

What did the beaver say to the tree?
It's been nice gnawing you.

What did the shoe say to the foot?
You're having me on.

Why did the belt go to jail?
Because it held up a pair of pants.

Twenty puppies were stolen from a pet shop. Police are warning people to look out for anyone selling hot dogs.

Why did the gangster kill his pet pig?
Because it squealed to the police.

Man: *'You were supposed to come around yesterday and fix my doorbell.'*
Electrician: *'I did. I rang twice but no one answered.'*

Who is the smelliest person in the world?
King Pong.

What do traffic wardens put on their sandwiches?
Traffic jam.

What kind of music does your father like to sing?
Pop music.

Where are English kings and queens crowned?
On the head.

What did Noah say as he was loading the animals?
Now I herd everything.

Why didn't the man die when he drank poison?
Because he was in the living room.

Why did the bat miss the train?
Because it spent too long hanging around.

Why was the bee's hair sticky?
Because he used a honey-comb!

What do bees wear to work?
Buzzness suits.

A man walked into a bar.
'Ouch!'

Where's your mum?
On holiday.
Jamaica?
No, she went of her own accord.

What did the little mountain say to the big mountain?
Hi Cliff!

Why do service stations always lock their bathrooms?
They are afraid someone might clean them.

Name three inventions that have helped man up in the world.
The escalator, the ladder and the alarm clock.

A man is lost in the desert. He crawls along, getting thirstier and thirstier. A man approaches with a case full of ties. 'Would you like to buy a tie?' the tie salesman asks. 'Water, water,' the other man pleads. 'Sorry, I only have ties.' Hours later, with the thirsty man near death, another man approaches. He too has ties but no water. The thirsty man keeps crawling. Almost dead, he sees in the distance a bar. He crawls to the entrance only to be stopped by a bouncer. 'Sorry sir,' the bouncer says. 'You can't get in without a tie.'

What's yellow and wears a mask?
The Lone Banana.

When is a car not a car?
When it has turned into a driveway.

My sister just married an Irishman.
Oh really.
No, O'Reilly.

Two horses are in a bar.
Horse 1: *'I see you had a good win on the track last week.'*
Horse 2: *'Thanks. I'm in pretty good form.'*

How do you make a Maltese cross?
Stomp on his foot.

Where was the Declaration of Independence signed?
At the bottom.

How many animals did Moses fit in the Ark?
None, it was Noah's Ark.

Where do you come from?
Australia.
Which part?
All of me.

What's the letter that ends everything?
The letter G.

How did the dentist become a brain surgeon?
His drill slipped.

Why did Henry VIII have so many wives?
He liked to chop and change.

Where does a sick ship go?
To the dock.

Why did the one-handed man cross the road?
He wanted to get to the second-hand shop!

Can you stand on your head?
No, my feet won't reach.

What's the difference between a bus driver and a cold?
One knows the stops, the other stops the nose.

What do you call a ship that lies on the bottom of the ocean and shakes?
A nervous WRECK!

When is a door not a door?
When it's ajar.

Did you hear about the two bodies cremated at the same time?
It was a dead heat.

What is the name of the detective who sings quietly to himself while solving crimes?
Sherlock Hums!

Boy...that last call home to Mum was a doozie

Why did E.T. have such big eyes?
Because he saw his phone bill.

What did the penny say to the other penny?
We make perfect cents.

How do you saw the sea in half?
With a sea-saw.

Who swings through the cake shop, yodelling?
Tarzipan.

The guy who invented the hokey pokey died but they couldn't get him into the coffin. His right leg was in, then his right leg was out, his right leg was...

What wears an anorak and pecks on trees?
Woody Wood Parka.

Did you hear about the unlucky sailor?
First he was shipwrecked, then he was rescued – by the Titanic.

That dress fits you like a glove. It sticks out in five places.

Did you hear about the criminal contortionist?
He turned himself in.

What's the easiest way to find a pin in your carpet?
Walk around in your bare feet.

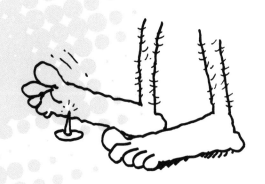

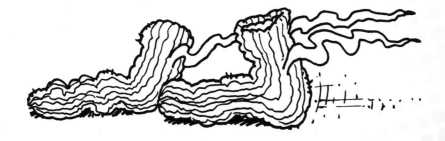

What's brown, hairy and has no legs but walks?
Dad's socks.

What did the stamp say to the envelope?
Stick with me and we will go places.

What are the four letters the dentist says when a patient visits him?
ICDK (I see decay)

What did the floor say to the desk?
I can see your drawers.

How do you make a hotdog stand?
Steal its chair!

Why was the baby pen crying?
Because its mum was doing a long sentence.

Where does this road go?
Nowhere. It stays right where it is.

A couple are in an airport queue.
Husband: *'We should have brought the dining room cabinet.'*
Wife: *'Why?'*
Husband: *'That's where I left the tickets.'*

Why does lightning shock people?
It doesn't know how to conduct itself.

What side of an apple is the left side?
The side that hasn't been eaten.

What did one wall say to the other wall?
I'll meet you at the corner.

What do you get if you jump into the Red Sea?
Wet.

What's easy to get into but hard to get out of?
Trouble.

How do we know that Moses was sick?
God gave him tablets.

Two chickens walk into a bar.
Barman: *'Sorry, we don't serve food in here.'*

Mother: *'Don't go too close to the lake. It's very deep.'*
Child: *'No it's not. It only goes up to the duck's middle.'*

Who delivers Christmas presents to the wrong houses?
Santa Flaws.

What were the gangster's final words?
What is that violin doing in my violin case?

A man walks into a bar with a skunk under his arm.
Barman: *'You can't bring that smelly thing in here.'*
Skunk: *'Sorry. I'll leave him outside.'*

What's the nearest thing to silver?
The Lone Ranger's bottom.

Police have arrested two kids, one for playing with fireworks, and one for stealing a battery. They charged one and let the other one off.

Mum, why isn't my nose twelve inches long?
Because then it would be a foot.

What's the hardest part about sky diving?
The ground!

Why did the bungee jumper take a holiday?
Because he was at the end of his rope.

What did one sole say to the other?
I think we're being followed by a couple of heels.

Why do toadstools grow so close together?
They don't need mushroom.

What has many rings but no fingers?
A telephone.

What do you call a man with an elephant on his head?
Squashed.

What's the definition of minimum?
A very small mother.

A plumber was called to fix a pipe at a doctor's house. After completing the job, the plumber handed over a large bill.

'That's outrageous,' said the doctor. *'I don't earn that much as a surgeon.'*

'Neither did I when I was a surgeon,' said the plumber.

What did one escalator say to the other?
I think I'm coming down with something.

Person 1: *'Pssst. Do you want to buy the genuine skull of Julius Caesar?'*
Person 2: *'You sold me his skull last week. Besides, that one is smaller.'*
Person 1: *'This is when he was a boy.'*

Which song is top of the Eskimo hit parade?
'There's No Business Like Snow Business.'

Why are gloves clumsy?
Because they're all fingers and thumbs.

Call me a taxi.
You're a taxi.

Home owner: *'Come here. I'll teach you to throw stones at my window.'*
Child: *'I already know how.'*

How did Noah steer the Ark at night?
He switched on the floodlights.

What has four wheels and flies?
A garbage truck.

What do you get if you cross the Atlantic with the Titanic?
About half way.

Where do you find baby soldiers?
In the infantry.

Can February March?
No. But April May.

Why was the archaeologist upset?
His job was in ruins!

What flowers grow under your nose?
Tulips.

What will go up a drainpipe down but won't go down a drainpipe up?
An umbrella.

I have five noses, seven ears and four mouths. What am I?
Very ugly.

What helps keep your teeth together?
Toothpaste.

Why did the toilet paper roll down the hill?
To get to the bottom.

How do you use an Egyptian doorbell?
Toot-and-come-in.

How did the Vikings send messages?
By Norse code.

How much does it cost for a pirate to get earrings?
A buccaneer!

Why do artists make lots of money?
Because they can draw their own wages.

My son writes for money.
Is he a novelist?
No, he's travelling. Every few days I get a letter asking for money.

What did one eye say to the other eye?
Something that smells has come between us.

Where are the Andes?
At the end of your armies.

Why do bagpipers walk when they play?
They're trying to get away from the noise.

What illness do retired pilots get?
Flu.

When do mathematicians die?
When their number's up.

What did the first mind reader say to the second mind reader?
You're all right, how am I?

What did one magnet say to the other magnet?
I find you very attractive.

What do you call a man who stands around and makes faces all day?
A clockmaker.

What did one toilet say to the other toilet?
You look a bit flushed!

When is a match not a match?
When it's alight.

What did the digital clock say to its mother?
Look ma, no hands.

What did the ground say to the rain?
If this keeps up, I'll be mud.

Where's Hadrian's Wall?
Around his garden.

Why did the car get a puncture?
There was a fork in the road.

Airline Steward: *'It is an offence to smoke on a plane. Anyone caught doing so will be asked to finish it outside.'*

What's the difference between a TV and a newspaper?
Ever tried swatting a fly with a TV?

A fish flounders into a bar, its tongue hanging out.
Barman: *'What can I get you?'*
Fish: *'Water, water.'*

Did you hear the one about the man that went into the cloning shop?
When he came out he was beside himself!

Hey.... grooovy legs man!

What do hippies do?
They hold your leggies on.

What has four legs and doesn't walk?
A table.

Why did the surfer stop surfing?
Because the sea weed.

Where does Tarzan buy his clothes?
At a jungle sale.

What do you call a snowman with a suntan?
A puddle!

What happens when the Queen burps?
She issues a royal pardon.

Why did the balloon burst?
Because it saw the soda pop!

What's that lyin' on the floor?
That's no lion, that's an elephant.

Officer, someone's stolen my wig.
Don't worry, we'll comb the area.

Why did the snowman dress up?
Because he was going to the snowball.

How did the comedian pass the time in hospital?
By telling sick jokes.

Why is it impossible to die of starvation in the desert?
Because of the sand which is there (sandwiches there).

When do you put a frog in your sister's bed?
When you can't find a mouse.

Sheriff: *'You're not allowed to fish here.'*
Boy: *'I'm not fishing. I'm giving my pet worm a bath.'*

Who steals from her grandma's house?
Little Red Robin Hood.

How do Eskimos dress?
As quickly as possible.

What's the easiest way to get on TV?
Sit on it.

Why did Polly put the kettle on?
She didn't have anything else to wear.

What's small, annoying and really ugly?
I don't know but it comes when I call my sister's name.

Why was the broom late?
It overswept.

What did the rug say to the floor?
Don't move, I've got you covered.

What's small and wobbly and sits in a pram?
A jelly baby.

Which trees are always sad?
Pine trees.

Hi MUM ...yeah I'm on TV!

RIDDLE ME TWICE

What has a bottom at the top?
A leg.

What's easier to give than receive?
Criticism.

What do you put in a barrel to make it lighter?
A hole.

What was the best thing before sliced bread?

What runs down the street but has no legs?
The kerb.

What washes up on very small beaches?
Microwaves!

What is there more of the less you see?
Darkness.

Why didn't the boy go to work in the wool factory?
Because he was too young to dye.

What's higher without the head than with it?
A pillow.

What did one angel say to the other angel?
Halo.

What did the dentist say to the golfer?
You've got a hole in one!

What bow can't be tied?
A rainbow!

What happened to the horse that swallowed the dollar?
He bucked.

Do these stairs take you to the third floor?
No, I'm afraid you'll have to walk!

How can you tell an undertaker?
By his grave manner.

What do elephants play marbles with?
Old bowling balls.

What has a hundred limbs but cannot walk?
A tree.

What is H2O4?
Drinking!

What is always behind the times?
The back of a watch.

What goes up and down but never moves?
A flight of stairs.

What kind of ship never sinks?
Friendship!

Which is the longest rope?
Europe!

What can't walk, but can run?
A river.

What word is always spelled incorrectly?
Incorrectly.

Why did the boy sit on his watch?
He wanted to be on time.

How do you make a pair of trousers last?
Make the coat first.

What is a forum?
One-um plus three-um.

Why are rivers lazy?
Because they never get off their beds.

Why are false teeth like stars?
They come out at night.

Why can't it rain for two days in a row?
Because there is a night in between.

What do you call a superb painting done by a rat?
A mouseterpiece!

Why was the mother flea so sad?
Because her children were going to the dogs.

What kind of sharks never eat women?
Man-eating sharks.

What can you hear but not see and only speaks when it is spoken to?
An echo.

If April showers bring May flowers, what do May flowers bring?
Pilgrims!

What can you hold but never touch?
A conversation.

If a 7-11 is open 24 hours a day, 365 days a year, why are there locks on the doors?

What is the fiercest flower in the garden?
The tiger lily.

What goes through water but doesn't get wet?
A ray of light.

What can you hold without touching?
Your breath.

What's grey and can't see well from either end?
A donkey with its eyes shut.

Why can't anyone stay angry with actors?
Because they always make up.

What goes around the house and in the house but never touches the house.
The sun.

What stays in the corner and travels all around the world?
A postage stamp.

What's green, has eight legs and would kill you if it fell on you from out of a tree?
A pool table.

How many seconds are there in a year?
12 . . . 2nd of January, 2nd of February . . . !

What goes all over the country but doesn't move?
The highway!

What cup can you never drink out of?
A hiccup.

Why does the ocean roar?
Because there are oysters in its bed!

Why did the girl buy a set of tools?
Everyone said she had a screw loose.

Why did the girl tear the calendar?
Because she wanted to take a month off.

What did Santa Claus' wife say during a thunderstorm?
Come and look at the rain, Dear.

What can be caught and heard, but never seen?
A remark.

What kind of cup can't hold water?
A cupcake.

What has two hands, no fingers, stands still and runs?
A clock.

What do you call a bee that is always complaining?
A grumble bee!

What goes all around a pasture but never moves?
A fence!

What starts with a P, ends with an E and has a million letters in it?
The Post Office!

What flies around all day but never goes anywhere?
A flag.

What is round and deep but could not be filled up by all the water in the world?
A colander.

If a horse loses its tail, where could it get another?
At a re-tail store.

What kind of star wears sunglasses?
A movie star.

URRGHH
Ever tried to hold a newspaper in one hand and put a ruler on it with the other to get the story straight?

Why did the girl keep a ruler on her newspaper?
Because she wanted to get the story straight.

What is the beginning of eternity, the end of time, the beginning of every ending?
The letter 'E'.

What gets bigger and bigger as you take more away from it?
A hole!

If a woman is born in China, grows up in Australia, goes to live in the United States and dies in New Orleans, what is she?
Dead.

Why were the arrows nervous?
Because they were all in a quiver.

When does a timid girl turn to stone?
When she becomes a little bolder (boulder)!

Why are good intentions like people who faint?
They need carrying out.

What has teeth but cannot eat?
A comb!

What goes up and does not come down?
Your age!

What did one bowling ball say to the other?
Don't stop me, I'm on a roll.

Whose fault is it when an axe hits a car?
No one's, it's an axe-ident.

What weapon was most feared by medieval knights?
A can opener.

What was the highest mountain before Mt Everest was discovered?
Mt Everest.

What did the burglar say to the lady who caught him stealing her silver?
I'm at your service, ma'am.

Why is a ladies' belt like a garbage truck?
Because it goes around and around to gather the waist.

What puzzles make you angry?
Crossword puzzles.

What question can you never answer yes to?
Are you asleep?

When Adam introduced himself to Eve, what three words did he use which read the same backward and forward?
Madam, I'm Adam.

What has four fingers and a thumb but is not a hand?
A glove!

Where were potatoes first found?
In the ground.

Where can you always find a helping hand?
At the end of your arm.

What sort of ring is always square?
A boxing ring!

Why do you go to bed?
Because the bed will not come to you.

Why did the dog cross the street?
To slobber on the other side.

Which room has no door, no windows, no floor, and no roof?
A mushroom!

What kind of coat can you put on only when it's wet?
A coat of paint.

When is it bad luck to be followed by a big black cat?
When you are a little grey mouse.

What's black when clean and white when dirty?
A blackboard.

What weighs more, a pound of lead or a pound of feathers?
They both weigh the same.

Why is the Mississippi such an unusual river?
It has four eyes and can't even see.

What has holes and holds water?
A sponge.

What did the mother sardine say to her baby when they saw a submarine?
Don't be scared. It's only a can of people.

What starts with an 'e', ends with an 'e', and only has 1 letter in it?
An envelope!

Why is milk the fastest thing in the world?
Because it's pasteurised before you see it.

What belongs to you but is used more by other people?
Your name.

What do you give a pig with a rash?
Oinkment!

EW!

Doctor, can a kid pull out his own tonsils.

Certainly not.

See Jimmy, I told you. Now put them back.

What do you get if you cross a burglar with a cement mixer?
A hardened criminal.

Why are basketball players never asked for dinner?
Because they're always dribbling!

Mummy, Mummy, what's a vampire?
Shut up and eat your soup before it clots.

If you want to be as scary and horrible as your father... you'll need to eat up all of your blood, like a good boy!

Why do little brothers chew with their mouths open?
Flies have got to live somewhere.

What has two grey legs and two brown legs?
An elephant with diarrhoea.

Mummy, Mummy, Dad has been run over by a steamroller.
Shut up and slide him under the door.

Mummy, Mummy, Sis has got a bruise.
Shut up and eat around it.

Mummy, Mummy, why is Dad running in zig zags?
Shut up and keep shooting.

What baseball position did the boy with no arms or legs play?
Home base.

What's Mozart up to now?
Decomposing.

Did you hear the one about the silly fox that got stuck in a trap?
She chewed off three legs and was still stuck.

How do you keep flies out of the kitchen?
Put a pile of manure in the living room!

Why did Piglet look in the toilet?
He was looking for Pooh.

What makes you seasick?
Your little brother's vomit.

What's twenty metres long and smells of urine?
Line dancing at the old people's home.

Why are sausages so bad mannered?
They spit in the frying pan.

Take that you filthy bad mannered brutes!!

How do you make a sausage roll?
Kick it down a hill.

Why do farts smell?
So that deaf people can appreciate them as well.

Mummy, Mummy, are you sure you bake bread this way?
Shut up and get back in. I can't close the oven door.

What's black and white and red all over?
A nun in a blender.

Mummy, Mummy, I hate my brother's guts.
Shut up and eat what's on your plate.

I just got a bunch of flowers for my wife.
Great swap.

What has fifty legs and can't walk?
Half a centipede.

What is the difference between broccoli and boogers?
Kids don't like to eat broccoli!

Mummy, Mummy, why can't we give Grandma a proper burial?
Shut up and keep flushing.

Did you hear the joke about the fart?
It stinks.

What do you call a boy who eats his mother and his father?
An orphan.

What has four legs and an arm?
A happy lion.

Mummy, Mummy, I don't want to go to New Zealand.
Shut up and keep swimming.

How do you make a hankie dance?
Put some boogie into it.

Why don't elephants pick their noses?
Because they don't know what to do with a 20 kilogram boogie.

Mummy, Mummy, I feel like a yo-yo.
Shut up and sit down … and down … and down…

What's green and red and goes at 100 kilometres per hour?
A frog in a blender.

Mummy, Mummy, I'm 16 years old. Don't you think I'm old enough to wear a bra now?
Shut up George.

Mummy, Mummy, Dad's going out.
Shut up and throw some more fuel on him.

Mummy, Mummy, Daddy's on fire.
Hurry up and get the marshmallows.

What's the last thing that goes through a bug's mind when he hits a car window?
His rear end.

What is the soft stuff between sharks' teeth?
Slow swimmers.

Why did the baker stop making donuts?
Because he was sick of the whole business.

What's another name for a snail?
A booger with a crash helmet.

Someone stole all the toilet seats from the police station. The officers have nothing to go on.

Mummy, Mummy, what are you doing with that axe?
Shut up and put your father's leg in the fridge.

What's green, sticky and smells like eucalyptus?
Koala vomit.

Mummy, Mummy, when are we going to have Grandma for dinner?
Shut up. We haven't finished eating your father yet.

What's thick and black and picks its nose?
Crude oil.

What's yellow and smells of bananas?
Monkey vomit.

What's the difference between a maggot and a cockroach?
Cockroaches crunch more when you eat them.

What did the cannibal have for breakfast?
Baked beings.

What did the first mate see in the toilet?
The captain's log.

If I had six grapefruit in one hand and seven in the other what would I have?
Very big hands.

Mummy, Mummy, Daddy just put Rover down.
I'm sure he had a good reason for it.
But he promised I could do it.

Mummy, Mummy, I can't find the dog's food.
Shut up and eat your stew.

Teacher: *'How was your holiday, Penny?'*
Penny: *'Great. My brother and I spent the whole time on the beach, burying Dad in the sand.'*
Teacher: *'That sounds like fun.'*
Penny: *'Mum says we can go back next year and find him.'*

There goes your Father again!

POP CORN

What did the baby corn say to the mother corn?

Where's pop corn?

Mummy, Mummy, can I play with Rover?

We've already dug him up three times this week.

What's the difference between an oral thermometer and a rectal thermometer?

The taste.

How can you tell when a moth farts?

He flies straight for a second.

Mummy, Mummy, Daddy's hammering on the roof again.

Shut up and drive a bit faster.

Mummy, Mummy, my head hurts.

Shut up and get away from the dartboard.

What's invisible and smells of carrots?

Bunny farts!!

Mummy, Mummy, why can't we buy a garbage disposal unit?

Shut up and keep chewing.

Mummy, Mummy, I've just chopped my foot off.

Then hop out of the kitchen, I've just mopped the floor.

Why was the sailor buried at sea?

Because he was dead.

Where do lepers shop?

At the second-hand store.

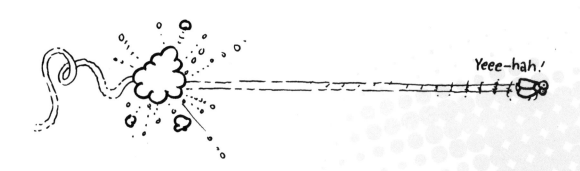

Yeee-hah!

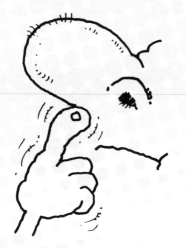

Mummy, Mummy, why do I keep going round in circles?
Shut up or I'll nail your other foot to the floor.

Mummy, Mummy, why are we pushing the car off the cliff?
Shut up or you'll wake your father.

What do you find up a clean nose?
Fingerprints.

What do you get if you cross an elephant with a box of laxatives?
Out of the way.

What did one plate say to the other plate?
Lunch is on me!

What's green and slimy and hangs from trees?
Giraffe boogie.

What's the difference between a worm and an apple?
Have you ever tried worm pie?

Three kids were playing in a park when a genie appeared. The genie said they could have one wish each, so long as they made the wish while coming down the slide.
The first kid slid down shouting, *'I want a big glass of lemonade.'* The second kid slid down shouting, *'I want a chocolate milkshake.'* The third kid slid down shouting, *'Weeeeee.'*

What's green, has two legs and sits on the end of your finger?
The boogieman.

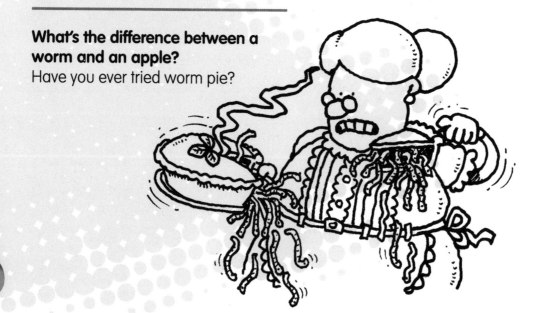

KNOCK KNOCK

Knock Knock. *Who's there?*
Theresa. *Theresa who?*
Theresa green.

Knock Knock. *Who's there?*
Cameron. *Cameron who?*
Cameron flash are what you need to take pictures when it's dark.

Knock Knock. *Who's there?*
Weirdo. *Weirdo who?*
Weirdo you think you're going?

Knock Knock. *Who's there?*
Police. *Police who?*
Police let me in.

Knock Knock. *Who's there?*
Barbie. *Barbie who?*
Barbie Q.

Knock Knock. *Who's there?*
House. *House who?*
House it going?

Knock Knock. *Who's there?*
Tuba. *Tuba who?*
Tuba toothpaste.

Knock Knock. *Who's there?*
Bach! *Bach who?*
Bach of chips!

Knock Knock. *Who's there?*
Jimmy! *Jimmy who?*
Jimmy a little kiss on the cheek!

COME ON...
OPEN UP....
this thing's heavy!

Knock Knock. *Who's there?*
X! *X who?*
X for breakfast!

Knock Knock. *Who's there?*
U-4! *U-4 who?*
U-4 me and me for you!

Knock Knock. *Who's there?*
Cantaloupe! *Cantaloupe who?*
Cantaloupe with you tonight!

Knock Knock. *Who's there?*
Adder. *Adder who?*
Adder you get in here?

Knock Knock. *Who's there?*
Yah. *Yah who?*
Ride 'em cowboy.

WOH THERE BUTTERCUP! Remember you're a dairy cow old girl!

Knock Knock. *Who's there?*
You. *You who?*
Did you call?

Knock Knock. *Who's there?*
Thistle. *Thistle who?*
Thistle be the last time I knock.

Knock Knock. *Who's there?*
Sam. *Sam who?*
Sam person who knocked yesterday.

Knock Knock. *Who's there?*
Olive. *Olive who?*
Olive in that house across the road.

Knock Knock. *Who's there?*
Oscar. *Oscar who?*
Oscar silly question get a silly answer.

Knock Knock. *Who's there?*
Orson. *Orson who?*
Orson cart!

Knock Knock. *Who's there?*
Irish. *Irish who?*
Irish I had a million dollars.

Knock Knock. *Who's there?*
Stopwatch. *Stopwatch who?*
Stopwatch you're doing and open this door!

Knock Knock. *Who's there?*
Alaska. *Alaska who?*
Alaska one more time . . . let me in!

Knock Knock. *Who's there?*
Weed. *Weed who?*
Weed better mow the lawn before it gets too long.

Knock Knock. *Who's there?*
Bee! *Bee who?*
Bee careful!

Knock Knock. *Who's there?*
Biafra! *Biafra who?*
Biafra'id, be very afraid!

Knock Knock. *Who's there?*
Abe! *Abe who?*
Abe C D E F G H . . .

Knock Knock. *Who's there?*
Jam! *Jam who?*
Jam mind, I'm trying to get out!

Knock Knock. *Who's there?*
Utah! *Utah who?*
Utah the rails and I'll mend the fence!

Knock Knock. *Who's there?*
Nicholas. *Nicholas who?*
Nicholas girls shouldn't climb trees.

Knock Knock. *Who's there?*
Gable! *Gable who?*
Gable to leap tall buildings in a single bound!

Knock Knock. *Who's there?*
Nana. *Nana who?*
Nana your business.

Knock Knock. *Who's there?*
Ken. *Ken who?*
Ken I come in, it's freezing out here.

Knock Knock. *Who's there?*
Madam. *Madam who?*
Madam foot got stuck in the door.

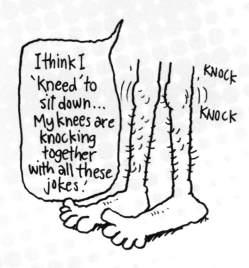

Knock Knock. *Who's there?*
Knee. *Knee who?*
Knee-d you ask?

Knock Knock. *Who's there?*
Dozen. *Dozen who?*
Dozen anyone know who I am?

Knock Knock. *Who's there?*
Celeste. *Celeste who?*
Celeste time I come round here.

Knock Knock. *Who's there?*
Shamp. *Shamp who?*
Why, do I have lice?

Knock Knock. *Who's there?*
Jamaica. *Jamaica who?*
Jamaica mistake?

Knock Knock. *Who's there?*
Army. *Army who?*
Army and you still friends?

Knock Knock. *Who's there?*
Ida. *Ida who?*
Ida know why I love you like I do.

Knock Knock. *Who's there?*
M-2. *M-2 who?*
M-2 tired to knock!

Knock Knock. *Who's there?*
Ben. *Ben who?*
Ben knocking on the door all afternoon!

Knock Knock. *Who's there?*
Phyllis. *Phyllis who?*
Phyllis a glass of water, will you?

Knock Knock. *Who's there?*
Howard. *Howard who?*
Howard I know?

That's a dreadful joke... I'm off!

QUACK QUACK QUACK QUACK

Knock Knock. *Who's there?*
Quacker! *Quacker who?*
Quacker 'nother bad joke and I'm leaving!

Knock Knock. *Who's there?*
Carmen! *Carmen who?*
Carmen get it!

Knock Knock. *Who's there?*
Carlotta! *Carlotta who?*
Carlotta trouble when it breaks down!

Knock Knock. *Who's there?*
C-2! *C-2 who?*
C-2 it that you don't forget my name next time!

Knock Knock. *Who's there?*
Beef! *Beef who?*
Bee fair now!

Knock Knock. *Who's there?*
Arthur! *Arthur who?*
Arthur any more at home like you!

Knock Knock. *Who's there?*
Cash. *Cash who?*
Are you a nut!

Knock Knock. *Who's there?*
Colin. *Colin who?*
Colin all cars. Colin all cars.

Knock Knock. *Who's there?*
Bea. *Bea who?*
Because I'm worth it.

Knock Knock. *Who's there?*
Aesop. *Aesop who?*
Aesop I saw a puddy cat.

Knock Knock. *Who's there?*
U-8! *U-8 who?*
U-8 my lunch!

BURRRPP Your lunch was delicious!

Knock Knock. *Who's there?*
Spell. *Spell who?*
W.H.O.

Knock Knock. *Who's there?*
Rose. *Rose who?*
Rose early to come and see you.

Knock Knock. *Who's there?*
Euripedes. *Euripedes who?*
Euripedes pants, Eumenides pants.

Knock Knock. *Who's there?*
Tish. *Tish who?*
Bless you!!

Knock Knock. *Who's there?*
Cows. *Cows who?*
No, cows moo!

Knock Knock. *Who's there?*
Watson. *Watson who?*
Watson TV tonight?

Knock Knock. *Who's there?*
Tex. *Tex who?*
Tex two to tango.

Knock Knock. *Who's there?*
Roach. *Roach who?*
Roach you a letter, but I didn't send it.

Knock Knock. *Who's there?*
Gotter. *Gotter who?*
Gotter go to the toilet.

Knock Knock. *Who's there?*
Cargo. *Cargo who?*
Cargo beep beep!

Knock Knock. *Who's there?*
Olive! *Olive who?*
Olive you!

Knock Knock. *Who's there?*
Abel! *Abel who?*
Abel seaman!

Knock Knock. *Who's there?*
Jaws! *Jaws who?*
Jaws truly!

Knock Knock. *Who's there?*
Zeke! *Zeke who?*
Zeke and you shall find!

Knock Knock. *Who's there?*
Carol! *Carol who?*
Carol go if you turn the ignition key!

Knock Knock. *Who's there?*
Ben! *Ben who?*
Ben away a long time!

Knock Knock. *Who's there?*
Patrick. *Patrick who?*
Patricked me into coming over.

Knock Knock. *Who's there?*
Olivia. *Olivia who?*
Olivia but I've lost my key.

Knock Knock. *Who's there?*
Mandy. *Mandy who?*
Mandy lifeboats, we're sinking.

Knock Knock. *Who's there?*
Kay. *Kay who?*
Kay sera sera.

Knock Knock. *Who's there?*
Fozzie. *Fozzie who?*
Fozzie hundredth time, my name is Nick.

Knock Knock. *Who's there?*
Ferdie. *Ferdie who?*
Ferdie last time open the door.

Knock Knock. *Who's there?*
X! *X who?*
X-tremely pleased to meet you!

Knock Knock. *Who's there?*
Abbot! *Abbot who?*
Abbot time you opened this door!

Knock Knock. *Who's there?*
Cornflakes. *Cornflakes who?*
I'll tell you tomorrow, it's a cereal.

Knock Knock. *Who's there?*
Alex. *Alex who?*
Alexplain later, just let me in.

Knock Knock. *Who's there?*
Abbot. *Abbot who?*
Abbot you don't know who this is!

Knock Knock. *Who's there?*
Brie! *Brie who?*
Brie me my supper!

Knock Knock. *Who's there?*
Adam! *Adam who?*
Adam up and tell me the total!

Knock Knock. *Who's there?*
Xena! *Xena who?*
Xena minute!

Knock Knock. *Who's there?*
Xenia! *Xenia who?*
Xenia stealing my cake!

Knock Knock. *Who's there?*
Jilly! *Jilly who?*
Jilly out here, so let me in!

Knock Knock. *Who's there?*
Zubin! *Zubin who?*
Zubin eating garlic again!

Knock Knock. *Who's there?*
My panther. *My panther who?*
My panther falling down.

Knock Knock. *Who's there?*
Fang. *Fang who?*
Fangs for opening the door.

Knock Knock. *Who's there?*
Ears. *Ears who?*
Ears some more knock knock jokes.

Knock Knock. *Who's there?*
Java. *Java who?*
Java dollar you can lend me?

Knock Knock. *Who's there?*
Hy. *Hy who?*
(sings) Hy ho, hi ho, it's off to work
we go.

Knock Knock. *Who's there?*
Xavier! *Xavier who?*
Xavier breath, I'm not leaving!

Knock Knock. *Who's there?*
Fantasy. *Fantasy who?*
Fantasy a walk on the beach.

Knock Knock. *Who's there?*
Lena. *Lena who?*
Lena little closer and I'll tell you.

Knock Knock. *Who's there?*
Moira. *Moira who?*
(sings) Moira see you, Moira want you.

Knock Knock. *Who's there?*
Betty. *Betty who?*
Betty late than never.

Knock Knock. *Who's there?*
Alison. *Alison who?*
Alison to the radio.

Knock Knock. *Who's there?*
Caterpillar. *Caterpillar who?*
Cat-er-pillar of feline society.

Knock Knock. *Who's there?*
Witches. *Witches who?*
Witches the way home?

Knock Knock. *Who's there?*
Sawyer. *Sawyer who?*
Sawyer lights on, thought I'd drop by.

Knock Knock. *Who's there?*
Turnip. *Turnip who?*
Turnip the heater, it's cold in here!

Knock Knock. *Who's there?*
Xavier! *Xavier who?*
Xavier money for a rainy day!

Knock Knock. *Who's there?*
Seymour. *Seymour who?*
You'll Seymour if you look through the window.

Knock Knock. *Who's there?*
Bridie! *Bridie who?*
(sings) Bridie light of the silvery moon!

Knock Knock. *Who's there?*
Mister. *Mister who?*
Mister last train home.

Knock Knock. *Who's there?*
Abyssinia! *Abyssinia who?*
Abyssinia when I get back!

Knock Knock. *Who's there?*
James! *James who?*
James people play!

Knock Knock. *Who's there?*
Razor. *Razor who?*
Razor hands, this is a stick-up.

Knock Knock. *Who's there?*
Tibet. *Tibet who?*
Early Tibet, early to rise.

Knock Knock. *Who's there?*
Nobody! *Nobody who?*
Just nobody!

Knock Knock. *Who's there?*
Zany! *Zany who?*
Zany body home?

Knock Knock. *Who's there?*
Sibyl. *Sibyl who?*
Sibyl Simon met a pieman going to the fair.

Knock Knock. *Who's there?*
Toyota. *Toyota who?*
Toyota be a law against knock knock jokes.

Knock Knock. *Who's there?*
Vault. *Vault who?*
(sings) Vault-sing Matilda.

Knock Knock. *Who's there?*
Who. *Who who?*
I can hear an echo.

Knock Knock. *Who's there?*
Scott. *Scott who?*
Scott nothing to do with you.

Knock Knock. *Who's there?*
Harley. *Harley who?*
Harley ever see you anymore.

Knock Knock. *Who's there?*
Nobel. *Nobel who?*
Nobel so I just knocked.

Knock Knock. *Who's there?*
Minnie. *Minnie who?*
Minnie people would like to know.

Knock Knock. *Who's there?*
Midas. *Midas who?*
Midas well let me in.

Knock Knock. *Who's there?*
German border patrol.
German border patrol who?
Ve vill ask ze questions.

Knock Knock. *Who's there?*
Canoe! *Canoe who?*
Canoe come out and play with me?

Knock Knock. *Who's there?*
Galway. *Galway who?*
Galway, you're annoying me.

Knock Knock. *Who's there?*
U-2! *U-2 who?*
U-2 can buy a brand new car for only $199 a month!

Knock Knock. *Who's there?*
Lionel. *Lionel who?*
Lionel bite you if you don't watch out.

Knock Knock. *Who's there?*
Boo. *Boo who?*
What are you crying about?

Knock Knock. *Who's there?*
Sigrid. *Sigrid who?*
Sigrid Service, now do exactly as I say.

Knock Knock. *Who's there?*
Kenya. *Kenya who?*
Kenya keep the noise down, some of us are trying to sleep.

Knock Knock. *Who's there?*
Passion. *Passion who?*
Just passion by and I thought I'd say hello.

Knock Knock. *Who's there?*
Vaughan. *Vaughan who?*
Vaughan day you'll let me in.

Knock Knock. *Who's there?*
Larva. *Larva who?*
I larva you.

Knock Knock. *Who's there?*
Igloo. *Igloo who?*
(sings) Igloo knew Suzie like I know Suzie.

Knock Knock. *Who's there?*
Abba! *Abba who?*
Abba banana!

Knock Knock. *Who's there?*
Figs. *Figs who?*
Figs the doorbell, it's been broken
for ages.

Knock Knock. *Who's there?*
Evan. *Evan who?*
Evan you should know who I am.

Knock Knock. *Who's there?*
Daryl. *Daryl who?*
Daryl never be another you.

Knock Knock. *Who's there?*
Eddie. *Eddie who?*
Eddie body home?

Knock Knock. *Who's there?*
Curry. *Curry who?*
Curry me back home please.

Knock Knock. *Who's there?*
Adair! *Adair who?*
Adair once, but I'm bald now!

Knock Knock. *Who's there?*
Burglar. *Burglar who?*
Burglars don't knock.

Knock Knock. *Who's there?*
Ahab. *Ahab who?*
Ahab to go to the toilet now.
Quick open the door.

Knock Knock. *Who's there?*
Acute. *Acute who?*
Acute little boy.

Knock Knock. *Who's there?*
Wenceslas. *Wenceslas who?*
Wenceslas bus home?

Knock Knock. *Who's there?*
Abbey! *Abbey who?*
Abbey stung me on the nose!

Knock Knock. *Who's there?*
Eiffel. *Eiffel who?*
Eiffel down.

Knock Knock. *Who's there?*
Gladys. *Gladys who?*
Gladys Saturday aren't you?

Knock Knock. *Who's there?*
Tank. *Tank who?*
You're welcome.

Knock Knock. *Who's there?*
Sancho. *Sancho who?*
Sancho a letter but you never replied.

Knock Knock. *Who's there?*
Adore. *Adore who?*
Adore is between us, open up.

Knock Knock. *Who's there?*
Haywood, Hugh and Harry.
Haywood, Hugh and Harry who?
Haywood Hugh Harry up and open the door!

Knock Knock. *Who's there?*
Canoe. *Canoe who?*
Canoe please open the door.

Knock Knock. *Who's there?*
Dishes. *Dishes who?*
Dishes a very bad joke!

Knock Knock. *Who's there?*
Howdy! *Howdy who?*
Howdy do that?

Knock Knock. *Who's there?*
Empty. *Empty who?*
Empty V (MTV).

Knock Knock. *Who's there?*
Boxer! *Boxer who?*
Boxer tricks!

Knock Knock. *Who's there?*
Bowl! *Bowl who?*
Bowl me over!

Knock Knock. *Who's there?*
Bernadette! *Bernadette who?*
Bernadette my lunch and now I'm starving!

Knock Knock. *Who's there?*
Waddle. *Waddle who?*
Waddle you give me to leave you alone?

Knock Knock. *Who's there?*
Haden. *Haden who?*
Haden seek.

Knock Knock. *Who's there?*
Fanny. *Fanny who?*
Fanny the way you keep asking 'Who's there?'

Knock Knock. *Who's there?*
Beth. *Beth who?*
Beth wisheth, thweetie.

Knock Knock. *Who's there?*
Bella! *Bella who?*
Bella bottom trousers!

Knock Knock. *Who's there?*
Effie. *Effie who?*
Effie'd known you were coming he'd have stayed at home.

Knock Knock. *Who's there?*
Dan. *Dan who?*
Dan Druff.

Knock Knock. *Who's there?*
Bassoon. *Bassoon who?*
Bassoon things will be better.

Knock Knock. *Who's there?*
A Fred. *A Fred who?*
Who's a Fred of the Big Bad Wolf?

BUTCHER LEFT LEG IN AND SHAKE IT ALL ABOUT

Knock Knock. *Who's there?*
Butcher! *Butcher who?*
Butcher left leg in, your left leg out!

Knock Knock. *Who's there?*
Butcher! *Butcher who?*
Butcher arms around me!

Knock Knock. *Who's there?*
Vitamin. *Vitamin who?*
Vitamin for a party!

Knock Knock. *Who's there?*
Wednesday. *Wednesday who?*
Wednesday saints go marching in!

Knock Knock. *Who's there?*
Willube. *Willube who?*
Willube my valentine?

Knock Knock. *Who's there?*
Still. *Still who?*
Still knocking.

Knock Knock. *Who's there?*
Artichokes. *Artichokes who?*
Artichokes when he eats too fast!

Knock Knock. *Who's there?*
Max. *Max who?*
Max no difference who it is – just open the door!

Knock Knock. *Who's there?*
Pencil. *Pencil who?*
If you don't wear a belt, your PENCIL fall down!

Knock Knock. *Who's there?*
Avon. *Avon who?*
Avon you to open the door.

Knock Knock. *Who's there?*
Butcher! *Butcher who?*
Butcher money where your mouth is!

Knock Knock. *Who's there?*
Caesar! *Caesar who?*
Caesar quickly, before she gets away!

Knock Knock. *Who's there?*
Ben Hur. *Ben Hur who?*
Ben Hur almost an hour so let me in.

Knock Knock. *Who's there?*
Albert. *Albert who?*
Albert you don't know who this is?

Knock Knock. *Who's there?*
Cattle. *Cattle who?*
Cattle always purr when you stroke it.

Knock Knock. *Who's there?*
Cheese. *Cheese who?*
Cheese a jolly good fellow.

Knock Knock. *Who's there?*
Danielle. *Danielle who?*
Danielle so loud, I can hear you.

Knock Knock. *Who's there?*
Caesar! *Caesar who?*
Caesar jolly good fellow!

Knock Knock. *Who's there?*
Germany. *Germany who?*
Germany people knock on your door?

Knock Knock. *Who's there?*
Ice cream! *Ice cream who?*
Ice cream, you scream!

Knock Knock. *Who's there?*
Shelby! *Shelby who?*
Shelby comin' round the mountain when she comes!

Knock Knock. *Who's there?*
Iran. *Iran who?*
Iran 25 laps around the track and boy, am I tired!

149

Knock Knock. *Who's there?*
Aardvark. *Aardvark who?*
Aardvark a million miles for one of your smiles!

Knock Knock. *Who's there?*
Celia. *Celia who?*
Celia later alligator.

Knock Knock. *Who's there?*
Snow. *Snow who?*
Snow good asking me.

Knock Knock. *Who's there?*
Baby Owl! *Baby Owl who?*
Baby Owl see you later, maybe I won't!

Knock Knock. *Who's there?*
Irish stew. *Irish stew who?*
Irish stew in the name of the law.

Knock Knock. *Who's there?*
Troy. *Troy who?*
Troy as I may, I can't reach the bell.

Knock Knock. *Who's there?*
Wilma. *Wilma who?*
Wilma dinner be ready soon?

Knock Knock. *Who's there?*
Justin. *Justin who?*
Justin time for lunch.

Knock Knock. *Who's there?*
Barbara! *Barbara who?*
Barbara black sheep, have you any wool!

Knock Knock. *Who's there?*
Robin. *Robin who?*
Robin you! So hand over your cash.

Knock Knock. *Who's there?*
Willy. *Willy who?*
Willy be ready soon?

Knock Knock. *Who's there?*
Freeze. *Freeze who?*
Freeze a jolly good fellow.

Knock Knock. *Who's there?*
Bean. *Bean who?*
Bean to any movies lately?

Knock Knock. *Who's there?*
Althea. *Althea who?*
Althea later, alligator.

Knock Knock. *Who's there?*
Wanda. *Wanda who?*
Wanda buy some cookies?

Knock Knock. *Who's there?*
Nobody. *Nobody who?*
No body, just a skeleton.

Knock Knock. *Who's there?*
Sarah. *Sarah who?*
Sarah doctor in the house? I don't feel so good.

Knock Knock. *Who's there?*
Cecil. *Cecil who?*
Cecil have music where ever she goes.

Knock Knock. *Who's there?*
Omar. *Omar who?*
Omar goodness gracious, I've got the wrong address.

Knock Knock. *Who's there?*
Offer. *Offer who?*
Offer gotten who I am.

Knock Knock. *Who's there?*
Major. *Major who?*
Major answer a knock knock joke.

Knock Knock. *Who's there?*
Stan. *Stan who?*
Stan back. I'm going to break the door down.

Knock Knock. *Who's there?*
Cook. *Cook who?*
Look at the time, it's one o'clock.

Knock Knock. *Who's there?*
Alaska. *Alaska who?*
Alaska no questions. You tella no lies.

Knock Knock. *Who's there?*
Zombies. *Zombies who?*
Zombies make honey, zombies just buzz around.

Knock Knock. *Who's there?*
Radio. *Radio who?*
Radio not, here I come!

Knock Knock. *Who's there?*
Satin. *Satin who?*
Who satin my chair?

Knock Knock. *Who's there?*
Butcher. *Butcher who?*
Butcher head on my shoulder!

Knock Knock. *Who's there?*
Arthur. *Arthur who?*
Arthur anymore jelly beans in the jar?

LOOK!!!

Knock Knock. *Who's there?*
Felix. *Felix who?*
Felix my ice cream, I'll lick his.

Knock Knock. *Who's there?*
Lettuce. *Lettuce who?*
Lettuce in, it's cold outside.

Knock Knock. *Who's there?*
Luke. *Luke who?*
Luke through the peephole and you'll see.

Knock Knock. *Who's there?*
Bacon! *Bacon who?*
Bacon a cake for your birthday!

Knock Knock. *Who's there?*
Dewayne! *Dewayne who?*
Dewayne the bathtub before I drown!

Knock Knock. *Who's there?*
Arch! *Arch who?*
Bless you!

Knock Knock. *Who's there?*
Maybelle. *Maybelle who?*
Maybelle doesn't work either.

Knock Knock. *Who's there?*
Lass. *Lass who?*
Are you a cowboy?

Knock Knock. *Who's there?*
Ivor. *Ivor who?*
Ivor you let me in or I'll break the door down.

Knock Knock. *Who's there?*
Datsun. *Datsun who?*
Datsun old joke.

Knock Knock. *Who's there?*
Beezer. *Beezer who?*
Beezer black and yellow and make honey.

Knock Knock. *Who's there?*
Turner. *Turner who?*
Turner round and you'll get a better look.

Knock Knock. *Who's there?*
Ralph. *Ralph who?*
Ralph! Ralph! Ralph! I'm a dog.

Knock Knock. *Who's there?*
Neil. *Neil who?*
Neil down and take a look through the letter slot.

Knock Knock. *Who's there?*
Liz. *Liz who?*
Lizen carefully to what I have to say.

Knock Knock. *Who's there?*
Little old lady. *Little old lady who?*
I didn't know you could yodel!

Knock Knock. *Who's there?*
Jeff. *Jeff who?*
Jeff in one ear, can you please speak a bit louder.

Knock Knock. *Who's there?*
Letter. *Letter who?*
Letter in or she'll knock the door down.

Knock Knock. *Who's there?*
Avenue. *Avenue who?*
Avenue heard these jokes before?

Knock Knock. *Who's there?*
Water. *Water who?*
Water friends for!

Knock Knock. *Who's there?*
Smore. *Smore who?*
Can I have smore marshmallows?

Knock Knock. *Who's there?*
Who. *Who who?*
What are you – an owl?

Knock Knock. *Who's there?*
Icon. *Icon who?*
Icon tell you another knock knock joke.
Do you want me to?

Knock Knock. *Who's there?*
Icy. *Icy who?*
I see your underwear.

Knock Knock. *Who's there?*
Wooden shoe. *Wooden shoe who?*
Wooden shoe like to know.

Knock Knock. *Who's there?*
Norma Lee. *Norma Lee who?*
Norma Lee I'd be at school, but I've
got the day off.

Knock Knock. *Who's there?*
Turnip. *Turnip who?*
Turnip for school tomorrow or there
will be trouble.

Knock Knock. *Who's there?*
Miniature. *Miniature who?*
Miniature let me in, I'll tell you.

Knock Knock. *Who's there?*
Dish. *Dish who?*
Dish is a stick-up.

Knock Knock. *Who's there?*
Accordion. *Accordion who?*
Accordion to the TV, it's going to rain tomorrow.

Knock Knock. *Who's there?*
Sombrero. *Sombrero who?*
(sings) Sombrero-ver the rainbow.

Knock Knock. *Who's there?*
Catch. *Catch who?*
God bless you!

Knock Knock. *Who's there?*
Leaf. *Leaf who?*
Leaf me alone.

Knock Knock. *Who's there?*
Rhoda. *Rhoda who?*
(sings) Row, Row, Rhoda boat.

Knock Knock. *Who's there?*
Tick. *Tick who?*
Tick 'em up, I'm a tongue-tied towboy.

Knock Knock. *Who's there?*
Despair. *Despair who?*
Despair tyre is flat.

Knock Knock. *Who's there?*
Closure. *Closure who?*
Closure mouth when you're eating!

Knock Knock. *Who's there?*
Waiter. *Waiter who?*
Waiter minute while I tie my shoe.

Knock Knock. *Who's there?*
William. *William who?*
William mind your own business?

Knock Knock. *Who's there?*
Winner. *Winner who?*
Winner you gonna get this door fixed?

LOVE AND HATE

What do you call an amorous insect?
A love bug!

I'll never forget the first time we met –
although I keep trying.

Every time I take my girlfriend out for a
meal, she eats her head off.
She looks better that way.

Do you think, Professor, that my
girlfriend should take up the piano as
a career?
*No, I think she should put down the lid
as a favour!*

**What do you call a hippo that believes
in peace, love and understanding?**
A hippie-potamus.

She's so ugly, when a wasp stings her,
it has to shut its eyes!

My dad once stopped a man ill-
treating a donkey.
It was a case of brotherly love . . .

First man: *'My girlfriend eats like a bird.'*
Second man: *'You mean she hardly
eats a thing?'*
First man: *'No, she eats slugs and
worms.'*

What did the bull say to the cow?
I'll love you for heifer and heifer.

**What did the undertaker say to his
girlfriend?**
Em-balmy about you!

What feature do witches love on their computers?
The spell-checker.

What does a boy monster do when a girl monster rolls her eyes at him?
He rolls them back to her.

What did the skeleton say to his girlfriend?
I love every bone in your body!

James: *'I call my girlfriend Peach.'*
John: *'Because she's soft, and beautiful as a peach?'*
James: *'No, because she's got a heart of stone.'*

Who were the world's shortest lovers?
Gnomeo and Juliet.

My cousin spent a lot on deodorant, until he found out people just didn't like him . . .

Why didn't the female frog lay eggs?
Because her husband spawned her affections.

What do you call a good-looking, kind and considerate monster?
A complete failure.

What happened when the snowman girl had a fight with her boyfriend?
She gave him the cold shoulder.

When Wally Witherspoon proposed to his girlfriend, she said, *'I love the simple things in life, Wally, but I don't want one of them for a husband!'*

First cannibal: *'My girlfriend's a tough old bird.'*
Second cannibal: *'You should have left her in the oven for another half-hour.'*

What do you get when you cross a vampire with a computer?
Love at first byte.

What did the rabbit give his girlfriend when they got engaged?
A 24-carrot ring.

History teacher: *'What's the best thing about history?'*
Mary: *'All the dates.'*

Why did they call the Cyclops a playboy?
Because he had an eye for the ladies!

Did you hear about the vampire who died of a broken heart?
She had loved in vein.

What's the difference between a peeping Tom and someone who's just got out of the bath!
One is rude and nosy. The other is nude and rosy!

Did you hear about the monster who sent his picture to a lonely hearts club?
They sent it back, saying they weren't that lonely.

Witch: *'When I'm old and ugly, will you still love me?'*
Wizard: *'I do, don't I?'*

What did the ghost buy for his wife?
A see-through nightie.

Boys fall in love with me at first sight.
I bet they change their minds when they look again.

What did the wizard say to his witch girlfriend?
Hello, gore-juice!

What would it take to make me look good?
A lot of distance between you and me.

I got a gold watch for my girlfriend.
I wish I could make a trade like that!

Why did the Invisible Man's wife understand him so well?
Because she could see right through him.

I'd love to go out with you, but my favourite commercial is on TV.

What happened when the young wizard met the young witch?
It was love at first fright.

What do girl snakes write on the bottom of their letters?
With love and hisses!

I can't understand why people say my girlfriend's legs look like matchsticks.
They do look like sticks – but they certainly don't match.

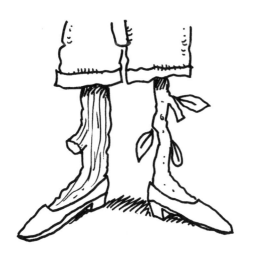

Who is a vampire likely to fall in love with?
The girl necks door.

'It's a pity you've gone on a hunger strike,' said the convict's girlfriend on visiting day.
'Why?' asked the convict.
'Because I've put a file in your cake!'

A woman woke her husband in the middle of the night.
'There's a burglar in the kitchen eating the cake I made this morning!' she said.
'Who should I call?' asked her husband. *'The police or an ambulance?'*

A woman was facing court, charged with wounding her husband.
'You're very lucky you're not facing a murder charge – why did you stab him over a hundred times?' asked the judge.
'I didn't know how to turn off the electric carving knife,' she replied.

'Can I go swimming now, Mum?' asked the child.
'No – there are sharks at this beach,' said his mother.
'Dad's swimming!'
Yes, he's got a million dollars' life insurance . . .'

ARE ZOO CRAZY?!?

Why wasn't the butterfly invited to the dance?
Because it was a moth ball.

Why do chickens watch TV?
For hentertainment.

Why did the zookeeper refuse to work in the elephant enclosure?
Because the work kept piling up.

Why can't you have a conversation with a goat?
Because it always butts in.

How do you know when there is an elephant in the oven?
You can't close the door.

What do you call a tall building that pigs work in?
A styscraper.

Where do sick ponies go?
To the horsepital.

What do you call a lamb with a machine gun?
Lambo.

What do you get if you sit under a cow?
A pat on the head.

Why did the chicken cross the basketball court?
He heard the referee calling fowls.

Why are skunks always arguing?
Because they like to make a big stink!

What's black and white and eats like a horse?
A zebra.

What's bright orange and sounds like a parrot?
A carrot!

What's tall, hairy, lives in the Himalayas and does 500 sit-ups a day?
The abdominal snowman!

What is a polygon?
A dead parrot.

What happened to the male bee that fell in love?
He got stuck on his honey.

What happened to the dog that swallowed the watch?
He got ticks.

What did the lioness say to the cub chasing the hunter?
Stop playing with your food.

What do lions say before they go out hunting for food?
Let us prey.

What's an eel's favourite song?
'Slip Sliding Away.'

What is a crowbar?
A place where crows go to get a drink!

How do fireflies start a race?
Ready, set, glow!

How many ants are needed to fill an apartment?
Ten-ants.

How do you know peanuts are fattening?
Have you ever seen a skinny elephant?

What's a pig's favourite ballet?
Swine Lake.

Where do elephants go on holidays?
Tuscany.

Why do elephants wear sneakers?
So they can sneak up on mice.

Did you hear about the naughty chicken?
It was eggspelled from school.

Where do bees go when they're sick?
To the waspital!

What do you call a baby whale?
A little squirt.

What do you call fourteen rabbits hopping backwards?
A receding hareline.

What do you call a fly with no wings?
A walk.

What do leopards say after lunch?
That sure hit the spots!

Who went into the tiger's lair and came out alive?
The tiger.

Why does a hummingbird hum?
It doesn't know the words!

What kind of cat shouldn't you play cards with?
A cheetah!

What bird is always out of breath?
A puffin.

I play Scrabble with my pet dog every night.
He must be clever.
I don't know about that. I usually beat him.

Where is the hottest place in the jungle?
Under a gorilla.

What do vultures always have for dinner?
Leftovers.

What's the difference between a mouse and an elephant?
About a tonne.

What do you get if you cross a tiger with a snowman?
Frostbite.

Who was the first deer astronaut?
Buck Rogers.

What do owls sing when it's raining?
Too wet to woo.

How do hens dance?
Chick to chick.

What kind of key doesn't unlock any doors?
A donkey.

How do you make a milkshake?
Give a cow a pogo stick.

What did the boa constrictor say to its victim?
I've got a crush on you.

Which bird can never be trusted?
A lyrebird.

What do bees do with their honey?
They cell it.

Where do tadpoles change into frogs?
The croakroom.

What do you give a dog with a fever?
Mustard, it's the best thing for a hot dog!

What's the difference between a unicorn and a lettuce?
One is a funny beast and the other a bunny feast.

What steps would you take if a bull chased you?
Big ones.

What do you call a group of boring, spotted dogs?
101 Dull-matians!

What cat has eight legs?
An octopus.

What do you call a Chinese cat that spies through windows?
A Peking tom.

What did the fish say when he swam into the wall?
Dam.

How do you stop a rhino from charging?
Take away its credit card!

How do you fit an elephant into a matchbox?
Take out the matches!

How do you fit a tiger into a matchbox?
Take out the elephant!

Why do buffaloes always travel in herds?
Because they're afraid of getting mugged by elephants.

How do ducks play tennis?
With a quacket.

What is a duck's favourite TV show?
The feather forecast.

What do you do if your chicken feels sick?
Give her an eggs-ray.

Which bird never grows up?
The minor bird.

What do you call a bee than buzzes quietly?
A mumble bee.

Why do bears have fur coats?
Because they can't get plastic raincoats in their size!

What do bees use to communicate with each other?
Their cell phones.

I've lost my dog.
Put an ad in the paper.
Don't be silly. He can't read.

Why are elephants big and grey?
Because if they were small and purple they would be grapes.

Why was the elephant standing on the marshmallow?
He didn't want to fall in the hot chocolate.

How do you know when there is an elephant in the fridge?
There are footprints in the butter.

Did you hear about the elephant who drank a bottle of rum?
He got trunk.

On which side does an eagle have most of its feathers?
On the outside.

165

What did one firefly say to the other before he left?
Bye! I'm glowing now!

What do you call two spiders who just got married?
Newlywebs!

How do you make a snake cry?
Take away its rattle!

How do we know that owls are smarter than chickens?
Have you ever heard of Kentucky-fried owl?

What do you get if you cross an eel with a shopper?
A slippery customer.

What do you get if you cross an electric eel with a sponge?
Shock absorbers.

What is a parrot's favourite game?
Hide and speak.

What do you call a mad flea?
A looney-tic!

Now you see it, now you don't. What could you be looking at?
A black cat walking over a zebra crossing!

What happens when ducks fly upside-down?
They quack up.

What's a lion's favourite food?
Baked beings.

What did the croaking frog say to her friend?
I think I've got a person in my throat.

How do you get an elephant into a car?
Open the door.

How does the elephant get out of the car?
The same way it got in.

Why is a snail stronger than an elephant?
A snail carries its house, and an elephant only carries its trunk!

Why was the kangaroo mad at her children?
Because they were jumping on the bed.

Why is the letter 'T' important to a stick insect?
Because without it, it would be a sick insect.

Why did the frog throw away the book?
Because he'd reddit (read it).

Why did the fish cross the sea?
To get to the other tide.

Who is emperor of all mice?
Julius Cheeser.

Why did the firefly get bad grades in school?
He wasn't very bright!

If a snake and an undertaker got married, what would they put on their towels?
Hiss and Hearse!

What game do elephants play in a Volkswagen?
Squash!

What is big, green and has a trunk?
An unripe elephant.

How does an elephant get down from a tree?
He sits on a leaf and waits for autumn.

Why do elephants' tusks stick out?
Because their parents can't afford braces!

Why didn't the piglets listen to their father?
Because he was a boar.

How do you make toast in the jungle?
Put your bread under a gorilla.

Why do frogs like beer?
Because it is made from hops.

What did the termite say when she saw that her friends had completely eaten a chair?
Wooden you know it!

What did one bee say to her nosy neighbour bee?
Mind your own bees' nest!

What's the best way to catch a monkey?
Climb a tree and act like a banana.

What has 500 pairs of sneakers, a ball and two hoops?
A centipede basketball team.

What's the best way to face a timid mouse?
Lie down in front of its mouse hole and cover your nose with cheese spread!

What do you get if you pour hot water down a rabbit hole?
Hot cross bunnies.

What's the difference between a tiger and a lion?
A tiger has the mane part missing.

Which language do birds speak?
Pigeon English.

What's the tallest yellow flower in the world?
A giraffodil.

Why are dolphins clever?
Because they live in schools.

Why are beavers so smart?
Because they gnaw everything.

Where would you weigh a whale?
At a whale-weigh station.

Which bird succeeds?
A budgie without teeth.

Which insects can tell the time?
Clockroaches.

Where did the cow go for its holiday?
Moo Zealand.

When is a brown dog not a brown dog?
When it's a greyhound.

What song do lions sing at Christmas?
Jungle bells.

What's green and dangerous?
A frog with a machine gun.

What do you give a sick bird?
Tweetment.

Where can you buy ancient elephants?
At a mammoth sale.

How do you hire a horse?
Put four bricks under his feet.

What does a porcupine have for lunch?
A hamburger with prickles.

What is more fantastic than a talking dog?
A spelling bee!

What are a bee's favourite soap operas?
The Bold & the Bee-utiful and Days of Our Hives!

What did the cat have for breakfast?
Mice Krispies.

Why was the chicken sick?
Because it had people pox.

Where do musical frogs perform?
At the Hopera House.

What kind of cat loves swimming?
An octopussy.

What do you call a bull taking a nap?
A bull dozer.

What is the biggest ant in the world?
An eleph-ant.

What's even bigger than that?
A gi-ant!

What is a narrow squeak?
A thin mouse!

When is a lion not a lion?
When he turns into his den.

What do elephants take when they can't sleep?
Trunkquilisers.

What do you call a travelling mosquito?
An itch-hiker.

What's black and white and red all over?
A sunburned zebra.

What's a sheep's favourite dessert?
A chocolate baaaaa.

What's a bee's favourite meal?
A humburger.

What does an educated owl say?
Whom.

What do you give to a sick snake?
An asp-rin.

Trouble sleeping? Here.... Take one of these and you'll sleep for a month!

What do you call an elephant in a telephone box?
Stuck.

What goes 99 bonk?
A centipede with a wooden leg.

Where do you find a no-legged dog?
Right where you left it.

What did the buffalo say to his son, when he went away on a long trip?
Bison.

Name an animal that lives in Lapland.
A reindeer.
Now name another.
Another reindeer.

How do cows count?
They use a cowculator.

What looks like half a cat?
The other half.

Which birds steal the soap from the bath?
Robber ducks.

What do cats eat as a special treat?
Mice creams.

What has an elephant's trunk, a tiger's stripes, a giraffe's neck and a baboon's bottom?
A zoo.

What's the definition of illegal?
A sick bird.

What happened when the owl lost his voice?
He didn't give a hoot.

Why do cows wear bells?
Because their horns don't work!

What do you get when you cross a dog with a vegetable?
A jack brussel.

What do get if you cross a centipede with a parrot?
A walkie-talkie.

What is white, fluffy and lives in the jungle?
A meringue-utan!

How do you get an elephant up an acorn tree?
Sit him on an acorn and wait twenty years.

What do elephants have that no other animal does?
Baby elephants.

What do get when you cross a dog and a cat?
An animal that chases itself.

How do you stop a pig from smelling?
Put a cork in his nose.

Why do snakes have forked tongues?
Because they can't use chopsticks.

What lives at the bottom of the sea with a six-gun?
Billy the Squid.

Why did the viper vipe her nose?
Because the adder ad' er' ankerchief.

Why did the fly fly?
Because the spider spied her.

What was the tortoise doing on the freeway?
About five kilometres an hour.

What do you get if you cross an alligator with a camera?
A snapshot.

What do cows listen to?
Moosic.

The hills are alive...
with the sound of mooosic

ON A HILL...SOMEWHERE IN AUSTRIA

What's a cow's favourite film?
The Sound of Moosic.

What goes 'oom, oom?'
A cow walking backwards.

Who is a snake's favourite singer?
Wriggley Houston.

What's Kermit the Frog's middle name?
The.

What's the difference between a bird and a fly?
A bird can fly but a fly can't bird.

What do you get if you cross a parrot with a shark?
A bird that will talk your ear off!

What's small, squeaks and hangs out in caves?
Stalagmice.

Who is a cow's favourite singer?
Moodonna.

What does a lion brush his mane with?
A catacomb.

What's another name for a clever duck?
A wise quacker!

Why are tigers and sergeants in the army alike?
They both wear the stripes.

Where does a pig go to pawn his watch?
A ham hock shop.

What do you call a crazy chicken?
A cuckoo cluck.

What do you get when you cross a monkey with a flower?
A chimp-pansy.

What's the biggest mouse in the world?
A hippopotamouse.

Why is the sky so high?
So birds won't bump their heads.

What did the caterpillar say to the butterfly?
You'll never get me up in one of those things.

What kinds of bees fight?
Rumble Bees!

Did you know that elephants never forget?
What do they have to remember!

What do you call a pony with a sore throat?
A little horse!

What's the best way to catch a rabbit?
Hide in the bushes and make a noise like lettuce.

What's the difference between an elephant and a flea?
An elephant can have fleas but a flea can't have elephants.

What's striped and goes around and around?
A zebra on a merry-go-round.

Are you a vegetarian because you love animals?
No, because I don't like plants.

What do you get if you cross a chicken with a yo-yo?
A bird that lays the same egg three times!

What's the difference between a buffalo and a bison?
You can't wash your hands in a buffalo.

What type of cats go bowling?
Alley cats.

What do you get from nervous cows?
Milk shakes.

What do termites eat for dessert?
Toothpicks.

What sort of music is played most in the jungle?
Snake, rattle and roll.

What do patriotic American monkeys wave on July 4th?
Star spangled bananas.

What has six legs and can fly long distances?
Three swallows.

Where do ants eat?
A restaur-ant.

What do frogs order in restaurants?
French Flies!

What do you get if you cross a bottle of water with an electric eel?
A bit of a shock!

What do you get if you cross a frog with a small dog?
A croaker spaniel.

What's black and white and goes around and around?
A penguin caught in a revolving door.

What did the duck say to the comedian after the show?
You really quacked me up!

What's a pelican's favourite dish?
Anything that fits the bill.

Did you put the cat out?
I didn't know it was on fire!

What sort of a bird steals from banks?
A robin.

What do you get when you cross an elephant with a fish?
Swimming trunks!

What type of food can't tortoises eat?
Fast food.

Where do pigs go when they die?
To the sty in the sky.

Which animals are best at maths?
Rabbits, because they're always multiplying.

Which bird can lift the heaviest weights?
The crane.

Which hen lays the longest?
A dead one.

Why did the rooster refuse to fight?
Because he was chicken.

What do you get when you cross a cat with a lemon?
A sour puss!

a romantic table for two in the corner next to the large rock amongst the coral

What does a crab use to call someone?
A shellular phone!

Why can't you play a practical joke on snakes?
Because they don't have a leg to pull.

Why did the fish jump out of the water?
Because the sea weed.

Why don't anteaters get sick?
Because they're full of antibodies.

Why should you never fight an echidna?
Because she will always win on points.

Why did the chicken cross the road?
To see the man laying bricks.

What goes 'dot, dot, dash, squeak'?
Mouse code.

How can you get a set of teeth put in for free?
Tease a lion.

What's the difference between a mosquito and a fly?
Try zipping up a mosquito!

What happens when a chimpanzee sprains his ankle?
He gets a monkey wrench.

What did the dog say when he was attacked by a tiger?
Nothing, dogs can't talk.

What has four legs and sees just as well from both ends?
A horse with his eyes closed.

What do you get when you cross a high chair and a bird?
A stool pigeon.

What do you get if you cross a cocker spaniel with a rooster and a poodle?
Cockerpoodledoo.

What do you call a Scottish parrot?
A Macaw.

What kind of tie does a pig wear?
A pigsty.

What is a dog's favourite food?
Anything that is on your plate!

How do you know that carrots are good for your eyesight?
Have you ever seen a rabbit wearing glasses?

What does an octopus wear when it's cold?
A coat of arms.

WASH DAY AT THE OCTOPUS' PLACE

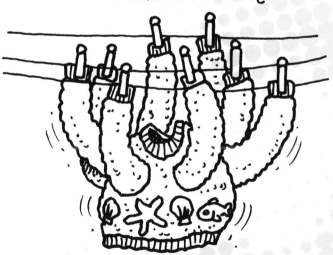

When do kangaroos celebrate their birthdays?
During leap year.

Why was the little bear spoilt?
Because he was panda'd to.

Why do elephants have Big Ears?
Because Noddy wouldn't pay the ransom.

Why did the elephant paint the bottoms of his feet yellow?
So he could hide upside down in custard.

Did you ever find an elephant in custard?
No.
It must work then!

Cow 1: *'Are you concerned about catching mad cow disease.'*
Cow 2: *'Not at all. I'm a sheep.'*

What's the difference between a dark sky and an injured lion?
One pours with rain, the other roars with pain.

Did you hear about the acrobatic snake?
He was in Monty Python's Flying Circus.

What are teenage giraffes told when they go on their first date?
No necking.

What did the cat say when it lost all its money?
I'm paw.

What do glowworms drink?
Light beer.

What do you call a cow that lives at the North Pole?
An eskimoo.

Customer: *'Have you got any dogs going cheap?'*
Pet Shop Owner: *'No, I'm afraid they all go woof.'*

THE BEST FOR LAST!

Silly Inventions

Waterproof teabags.

A parachute that opens on impact.

A chocolate teapot.

A one-way escalator.

Black windows.

An ejector seat on a helicopter.

A left-handed screwdriver.

A fly screen on a submarine.

An ashtray for a motorbike.

A bikini for Eskimos.

A lead balloon.

Underwear for kilt wearers.

A solar-powered torch.

Sugar cube fishing bait.

Rubber nails.

Non-stick glue.

A mirror for ghosts.

one minute it was there ...I turned around... and it was gone...

What did the farmer say when he lost his tractor?
Where's my tractor?

What's red and hangs in an orange tree?
A silly strawberry.

What's green and sings?
Elvis Parsley.

What colour is a hiccup?
Burple.

What's black and white and rolls down a hill?
A penguin.

What's black and white and laughs?
The penguin who pushed the other one.

Why did the fool climb the glass wall?
To see what was on the other side!

What do you do with a blue monster?
Try to cheer him up a bit.

What's a sick joke?
Something that comes up in conversation.

How does Frankenstein eat?
He bolts his food down.

Where do ghosts go to learn to frighten people?
Swooniversity.

What is a volcano?
A mountain with the hiccups.

Hairdresser: *'Would you like a haircut?'*
Boy: *'No, I'd like them all cut.'*

Why did the fool buy a chess set?
He was saving it for a brainy day.

Why did the fool cross the road?
To get to the middle.

How do you keep a fool in suspense?
I'll tell you tomorrow!

How did the silly boy break his arm while raking leaves?
He fell out of the tree!

How many optimists does it take to change a light bulb?
None, they reckon the power will come on without a bulb.

What do you call a shy sheep?
Baaaashful.

Which vegetables have toes at the end?
Tomatoes and potatoes.

What do you call banana skins that you wear on your feet?
Slippers.

What do you call a space magician?
A flying sorcerer!

What happened to the foolish tap dancer?
She fell in the sink.

How do you confuse an idiot?
Put him in a round room and tell him to sit in the corner!

How many archaeologists does it take to change a light bulb?
Five, one to change it, the others to argue about the age of the old one.

How many bureaucrats does it take to change a light bulb?
None, until the correct form has been filled out – in triplicate.

How many pessimists does it take to change a light bulb?
It doesn't matter, they reckon a new one will blow straight away anyway.

Instead of drinking from the fountain of knowledge, you just gargled.

What's green and hard?
A frog that lifts weights.

What's yellow and square?
A tomato in disguise.

How can you help a hungry cannibal?
Give him a hand.

What's purple, 5000 years old and 400 kilometres long?
The Grape Wall of China.

How did the fool fall on the floor?
He tripped over the cordless phone!

What's that on your shoulder?
A birthmark.
How long have you had it?

What is red, sweet and bites people?
A jampire!

What do you mean by telling everyone that I'm an idiot?
I'm sorry, I didn't know it was supposed to be a secret!

Why did the fool sleep under his car?
So he would wake up oily in the morning.

Why did the boy take his own toilet paper to the birthday party?
Because he was a party pooper.

How do you know when a fool has been making chocolate chip cookies?
There are M&M shells on the floor!

Why did the monster paint himself in rainbow-coloured stripes?
He wanted to hide in a pencil case.

What's red on the outside and green inside?
A dinosaur wearing red pyjamas.

Did you hear that he was buried face down?
Why?
So he could see where he was going.

What's grey, has four legs and a trunk?
A mouse going on holiday.

The cost of living is so high.
So why do you bother living?

Why did the dinosaur not cross the road?
It was extinct.

A ghost walks into a bar.
Bartender: *'Sorry, we don't serve spirits here.'*

Did you hear about the vampire comedian?
He specialised in biting satire.

What do sea monsters eat?
Fish and ships.

Waiter, there's a cockroach in my soup.
Sorry sir, we're all out of flies.

What do you do with a mouse that squeaks?
You oil him.

Why did the dinosaur cross the road?
Because there were no chickens.

Why did your sister put her socks on inside out?
Because there was a hole on the outside.

My sister went on a crash diet.
Is that why she looks like such a wreck?

My sister is so dim that she thinks a cartoon is something you sing in the car!

My sister is so dumb that she thinks a buttress is a female goat!

How can you tell if a vampire has a cold?
He starts coffin!

Why did the ghost go to jail?
For driving without due scare and attention.

What trees do ghosts like best?
Ceme-trees.

Why don't nuts go out at night?
Because they don't want to be assaulted.

How does a witch tell the time?
With a witch watch!

Why was the musician in prison?
Because he was always getting into treble.

How do dinosaurs pay their bills?
With Tyrannosaurus Cheques.

Why did the dinosaur cross the road?
What road?

What dinosaur can't stay out in the rain?
Stegosaur-rust!

What did the egg say to the dinosaur?
You're egg-stinct.

What did King Kong say when his sister had a baby?
Well I'll be a monkey's uncle.

What do Native American ghosts sleep in?
A creepy teepee!

Why do ghosts go to parties?
To have a wail of a time.

What is a runner's favourite subject in school?
Jog-raphy!

Name a tennis player's favourite city.
Volley Wood.

Who won the race between two balls of string?
They were tied!

What part of a football field smells the best?
The scenter spot!

What creates the most housework in alien homes?
Stardust.

What is an English teacher's favourite fruit?
The Grapes of Wrath.

What did the witch say to the vampire?
Get a life.

Why did Dracula take some medicine?
To stop his coffin.

How do you make seven an even number?
Take off the s.

Name three famous poles.
North, south and tad.

What illness do martial artists get?
Kung Flu.

What do you call the cannibal who ate her father's sister?
An aunt-eater!

Brother: *'Where was Solomon's temple?'*
Sister: *'On either side of his head.'*

Why do gingerbread men wear trousers?
Because they have crummy legs.

How do you make an egg laugh?
Tell it a yolk.

What's rhubarb?
Embarrassed celery.

What's green and short and goes camping?
A boy sprout.

Who is the most feared animal of all?
Attila the hen.

Why did the chicken join the band?
Because it had drumsticks.

Where do soccer players dance?
At a football.

What do you get when you cross a dinosaur with a pig?
Jurassic Pork.

Geography teacher: *'What's the coldest country in the world?'*
Student: *'Chile.'*

Simple Simon was writing a geography essay for his teacher. It began like this: *The people who live in Paris are called parasites.*

Science teacher: *'What are nitrates?'*
Student: *'Cheaper than day rates.'*

What do you call a blind dinosaur?
Do-ya-think-he-saw-us?

What's the difference between a dinosaur and a sandwich?
A sandwich doesn't weigh five tonnes.

What is the smelliest game in the world?
Ping-Pong!

What do you call a sleeping monster who won't keep quiet?
Frankensnore.

What does a ghost have to get before he can scare anyone?
A haunting licence.

Why did Dr Jekyll cross the road?
To get to the other Hyde!

Where does a monster go on Saturday nights?
Somewhere he can boogie!

How do dinosaurs pass exams?
With extinction.

What do you get if you cross a dinosaur with a kangaroo?
A huge animal that causes earthquakes wherever it hops.

Why do they have a fence around the graveyard?
Everyone is dying to get in!

What is a vampire's favourite kind of coffee?
De-coffin-ated!

What did one skeleton say to the other?
If we had any guts we'd get out of here!

What is Count Dracula's favourite snack?
A fangfurter!

Where would you get a job playing an elastic trumpet?
In a rubber band!

Did you hear about the two fat men who ran a marathon?
One ran in short bursts, the other ran in burst shorts.

How can you tell when there's a fool on an oil rig?
He's the one throwing bread to the helicopters.

What did the fool call his pet zebra?
Spot.

Did you hear about the fool who did bird impressions?
He ate worms.

Why did the fool break into two windows?
One to go in and the other to go out.

What do you get if you cross Bambi with a ghost?
Bamboo.

Why did the man cross a chicken with an octopus?
So everyone in his family could have a leg each.

What would you get if you crossed a hunting dog with a journalist?
A news hound.

How does a lion say hi to other animals?
Pleased to eat you!

Why did the insects drop the centipede from their football team?
He took too long to put on his shoes!

What happened to the leopard who took four baths every day?
Within a week he was spotless.

George is the type of boy that his mother doesn't want him to hang around with . . .

Are you all nice and tidy to go out George? Have you got a clean hanky and underpants?

What's black and very noisy?
A crow with a drum set.

Did you hear about the girl who got her brother a birthday cake, but then couldn't figure out how to get the cake in the typewriter to write 'Happy Birthday'?

What's extinct and works in rodeos?
Bronco-saurus.

What do you get if you cross a giraffe with a porcupine?
A 9-metre toothbrush.

What's the same size and shape as an elephant but weighs nothing?
An elephant's shadow.

What do you call a baby whale that never stops crying?
A little blubber.

How do you know when it's raining cats and dogs?
You step into a poodle.

Did you hear about the time Eddie's sister tried to make a birthday cake?
The candles melted in the oven.

Why did your sister keep running around her bed?
Because she was trying to catch up on her sleep!

History teacher: *'What's a Grecian urn?'*
Student: *'About $500 a week.'*

There's no point in telling some people a joke with a double meaning. They wouldn't understand either of them!

What do you call a cow riding a skateboard?
A cow-tastrophe about to happen.

What does a ghost read every day?
His horrorscope.

What is a ghost's favourite dessert?
Boo-berry pie with I-scream!

When do ghosts usually appear?
Just before someone screams!

What's the best way to call a Tyrannosaurus Rex?
Long distance!

What do you call a group of people that dig for bones?
A skeleton crew.

What do you get if you cross a pig with a zebra?
Striped sausages.

What do you call the red stuff between an elephant's toes?
A slow explorer.

What don't more dinosaurs join the police force?
They can't hide behind billboards.

What do vampires cross the sea in?
Blood vessels.

What do devils drink?
Demonade.

What do you call a three metre tall monster?
Shorty!

Why aren't vampires welcome in blood banks?
Because they only make withdrawals.

What do you get when you cross a dinosaur with explosives?
Dino-mite.

Do zombies like the dark?
Of corpse they do.

What did the alien say to the plant?
Take me to your weeder.

Who is the best dancer at a monster party?
The Boogie Man!

What do little zombies play?
Corpses and robbers.

What do vegetarian cannibals eat?
Swedes.

What does an undertaker take before starting work?
A stiff drink.

What happened when the gravediggers went on strike?
Their job was done by a skeleton crew.

What's a vampire's favourite dance?
The fangdango.

Which ghost is President of France?
Charles de Ghoul.

Why is Count Dracula skinny?
Because he eats necks to nothing.

The cat that made off with the mouse ... and the computer

Why did the cat sit on the computer?
To keep an eye on the mouse.

Mum: *'Why are you scratching, Jamie?'*
Jamie: *'Because no one else knows where I itch.'*

Why did the boy carry a clock and a bird on Halloween?
It was for tick or tweet!

How did the invisible boy upset his mother?
He kept appearing.

Roy: *'They say ignorance is bliss.'*
Rita: *'Then you should be the happiest boy in the world!'*

Why did the lazy boy get a job in a bakery?
Because he wanted to loaf around!

Big brother: *'That planet over there is Mars.'*
Little brother: *'Then that other one must be Pa's.'*

Why did Matt's bicycle keep falling over?
Because it was two tired.

How does a witch doctor ask a girl to dance?
Voodoo like to dance with me?

Why did the girl take a load of hay to bed?
To feed her nightmare.

Why did the silly girl spend two weeks in a revolving door?
Because she was looking for the doorknob.

Why do dinosaurs have wrinkles in their knees?
Because they've stayed in the bath too long.

If you stay in the bath too long, you'll go as wrinkly as a prune!